John Stuart Mill
THEISM

Edited with an Introduction by
RICHARD TAYLOR
Associate Professor of Philosophy, Brown University

The Library of Liberal Arts
published by

THE **BOBBS-MERRILL** COMPANY, INC.
A SUBSIDIARY OF HOWARD W. SAMS & CO., INC.
Publishers • INDIANAPOLIS • NEW YORK

Printed in the United States of America

The Library of Liberal Arts

[NUMBER SIXTY-FOUR]

John Stuart Mill

THEISM

The Library of Liberal Arts
OSKAR PIEST, FOUNDER

The Library of Liberal Arts

CONTENTS

JOHN STUART MILL: A CHRONOLOGY — vi

EDITOR'S INTRODUCTION — vii

NOTE ON THE TEXT — xix

SELECTED BIBLIOGRAPHY — xx

THEISM

PART ONE

Introduction — 3

Theism — 6

The Evidences of Theism — 10

Argument for a First Cause — 12

Argument from the General Consent of Mankind — 20

The Argument from Consciousness — 24

The Argument from Marks of Design in Nature — 27

PART TWO: *Attributes* — 33

PART THREE: *Immortality* — 46

PART FOUR: *Revelation* — 57

PART FIVE: *General Result* — 77

APPENDIX: *The Moral Attributes of God* — 89

INDEX — 97

JOHN STUART MILL: A CHRONOLOGY

1806	May 20, born at Pentonville, London
1809	Began study of Greek language and literature
1814	Began study of Latin, Euclid and algebra
1818	Began study of Aristotle's logical works and Scholastic logic
1819	Began study of political economy under his father
1820–21	Sojourn in France with Sir Samuel Bentham
1822	Entered as clerk in examiner's office, East India Company
1822	Established the "Utilitarian Society"
1826–c. 30	Period of disillusionment and depression
1828	Promoted to Assistant Examiner of East India Company
1835	Became editor of new *London Review*
1836–40	Edited and owned the *London and Westminister Review*
1851	Married Mrs. Harriet Hardy Taylor
1856–58	Chief of examiner's office, East India Company
1858	Death of Mrs. Mill
1865	Elected to Parliament from Westminster
1868	Defeated in election, retired to Avignon
1873	May 8, died at Avignon

EDITOR'S INTRODUCTION

John Stuart Mill (1806-1873) was virtually unique in his generation, and would be hardly less so in ours, in having passed to maturity with no deliberately inculcated religious influences, the remarkable education he received from his father simply omitting both religious and anti-religious instruction altogether. He thus, unlike many distinguished men of his day, never lost his religion, simply because he had none to lose, and he was able, in his writings, to view the Christianity of his contemporaries in much the same detached way in which we consider the religious and moral concepts of antiquity, with a disposition neither to defend nor to attack them, but simply to consider them on their own merits, in the light of such knowledge as we have from experience, science and philosophy, and without any pretensions to special revelations from the Almighty.

His *Theism,* the third of his *Three Essays on Religion,* was the last major writing that he completed, and was published the year after his death. It stands even today as an epitome of natural, as contrasted with revealed, religion, culminating a tradition which included such works as Samuel Clarke's *A Demonstration of the Being and Attributes of God* (1705), Bishop Butler's *Analogy of Religion* (1736), David Hume's *Dialogues Concerning Natural Religion* (1779), and William Paley's *Natural Theology* (1802).

By "natural religion" is meant the elaboration of certain doctrines customarily associated with religion, but entirely upon the evidence of human experience and the light of human reason. It treats religion, as Mill himself expresses it, "as a strictly scientific question," testing its claims "by the same scientific methods, and on the same principles as those of any of the speculative conclusions drawn by physical science." Traditional or revealed religion, on the other hand, regards its doctrines, or such of them as are alleged to have been at some time revealed to men by God or to rest upon a tradition considered sufficient to establish their divine character, as *given* once for all, and the task of the theologian is then, not to show that they are true—this being already accepted on faith—but to adduce further doctrines from them and bring them to bear upon the usual human problems of faith and morals. A Christian theologian can, for example, use as a *premise,* implicit in Scripture and hence requiring no reasoned justification, the proposition that God, though one, is in three persons—the Father or Creator, Jesus as God incarnate, and the Holy Ghost—and reason from this and similar doctrines to others which then ultimately constitute a part of orthodox belief. The philosopher of natural religion, however, cannot introduce a proposition such as this, for, as orthodox theology itself asserts, it is not only unprovable, but not even intelligible to human reason. Natural religion, accordingly, is of particular concern to those who are profoundly interested in the questions of religion, but who lack the gift of faith to receive without scruple any body of doctrines as having been once indubitably revealed by God.

The initial questions of natural religion concern, of course, the existence of God, and in this, as in every other problem he discusses, Mill distinguishes two questions: (1) What conceptions of God (or of gods) are consistent with what we know from science and from ordinary experience? and (2) Is any God (or gods) in fact shown, by what we know, to exist, or probably to exist? It would, for instance, be quite *consistent* with what we know to hold that the world is the working out of two supreme beings, one supremely good and the other supremely bad, as the Manichaeans maintained, and as many Christians have in effect believed; but there is no evidence that this belief, though consistent, is in fact true. Interestingly, the one claim which Mill singles out as inconsistent with what we know from experience, and hence as not possibly true, is the orthodox Christian conception of a God who is omnipotent, omniscient and benevolent—that is, infinite with respect to these attributes—and who yet governs with a variable will, susceptible to influence by human prayers and petitions, capable of approval and anger, and sometimes frustrated by the acts of his own creatures. Mill regards this as not only self-inconsistent, but inconsistent with the world that we actually find, considered as God's creation.

Yet Mill did believe, on the evidence of science and his own observations, that there does exist a God or Demiurge, that he is, though finite, in important respects not unlike the traditional Christian and Jewish conception of him, that the world is the result of divine plan, and that there is but one God. His reasons for endorsing monotheism are significant, for as he himself points out, polytheism is the far more natural and prevalent belief, and even in those traditions where monotheism is most vigorously asserted, one usually finds that its votaries pay reverence to a varied assortment of superhuman beings—angels, for instance, and other quasi-divine personages—only withholding from them the *name* "gods." David Hume had, moreover, thought himself to have shown, in one of the strongest arguments of the *Dialogues Concerning Natural Religion* [1] that *if* the world exhibits evidence of divine origin, as Mill believed it does, then, on the principle of strict analogy to human artifacts, it must be the product of countless gods and godlings, none of them very inspiring or worthy of worship—and Hume thought, as most would agree, that it would be preferable to have no religion at all than to erect such a "wild and unsettled" theology as this. Mill argues, however, that if, as he believed, the world shows signs of divine plan, then it is evidently the result of a single plan; for it is a single interconnected whole, governed throughout by the same natural laws, such that a change anywhere is capable of having effects everywhere, and not a world whose different parts go their separate ways, each under the reign of a separate divinity acting independently of others. Monotheism, accordingly, he considers the only form of theism which can claim any scientific ground.

The only argument for God that Mill thought to have any

[1] Part V.

weight is the celebrated argument from design—probably the oldest, clearest and most persuasive of any—rejected by both Hume and Kant only with reluctance.[2] Traditionally, this has been considered to be an argument from analogy; that is, a theory resting on the similarity between natural productions and human artifacts, and concluding from this a similarity of cause, viz., intelligence. Paley's version of it,[3] with which nearly everyone is familiar, is that if one were to find some such object as a watch or camera in some presumably uninhabited place—for instance, on the moon, if men ever get there—then he could infallibly conclude that the place was not uninhabited after all. Indeed, even the discovery of crude arrowheads would warrant this inference. But similarly, we find in nature things very much like watches and cameras—the human eye, for example, or man's mind—which are, however, vastly more complex and ingenious than human productions. We may, therefore, conclude that these too are the product of intelligence and, since not of human intelligence, then of divine.

This argument has some force, but not much, for the similarity of natural productions to human artifacts might be merely coincidental (as in the case of snowflakes, with their intricate and lovely designs), implying nothing at all concerning their ultimate origin. But it is perhaps Mill's most worthwhile contribution to this problem to point out that there can be added to this somewhat weak analogy a real induction which, though admittedly not probative, is nevertheless immensely stronger than analogy. What we find, that is to say, is not simply a similarity, possibly accidental, between things in nature, such as animal organisms, and works of intelligence, but a similarity with respect to the very characteristics which, we have learned from experience, causally depend upon intelligence. The parts of the eye, for instance, have no significant

[2] Because of the enigmatic conclusion to the *Dialogues Concerning Natural Religion,* Hume's real attitude toward this argument is controversial.

[3] *Natural Theology,* ch. 1.

similarity to each other, except that they are organized in such a way that together they subserve the purpose of vision. But as soon as *purpose* is introduced into the description of anything, we are tacitly presupposing an intention or will of a maker, and describing something of which not merely the existence but the arrangement or order as well depend upon an antecedent will and idea, and hence upon an intelligence.

Probably the only plausible alternative to this line of thought is Darwinism, and it is significant that Mill was familiar with that speculation. It is important to note, though, that the alternative is not, as is so often represented, "evolution," for Mill himself accepted, as obvious and beyond controversy, the theory of evolution—that is, the supposition that the present state of the world is the result of an enormously long and gradual process of development. This in itself explains nothing whatever. Darwinism seeks to *account* for that development by the hypothesis of natural selection through the survival of the fittest, and it is that purported *explanation* of evolution which Mill thinks improbable, though by no means absurd, and leaves to whatever fate the future may hold for it. The issue has not been settled since Mill's day, and indeed seems to have become more filled with doubt, the increase of knowledge in the realms of heredity and mutations apparently casting more darkness than light upon these problems.

With regard to God's attributes, Mill finds it easier to say with finality which ones must be lacking than which ones may be affirmed. Thus, if design is a fact—and Mill regards it as the only fact upon which theism can rest—then the infinite power traditionally ascribed to God is positively ruled out by that fact, as Kant had pointed out, though immense power is not. Similarly, God may have infinite wisdom, but there is no evidence from nature for thinking so. In so far as God's purposes can be inferred from nature, the chief one seems to be nothing more noble than the preservation of his creatures—of the world for a great but still finite time, of species for a long but lesser time, and of individuals for but a brief span. There may also be some justification for saying that God desires the well-being or happiness of all sentient things, inasmuch as the things most suggestive of design do in fact tend, more or less, to that result; but this cannot possibly be considered his chief purpose, and in any case *ought* not to be thought so by pious people—for if this were considered God's main intention, the result, in the light of the whole of history, has clearly fallen far short of success, with whatever reflection this might cast upon the Almighty. With regard to God's supposed justice, the evidence of nature is a total blank, there being no sign anywhere either of justice or injustice other than what men themselves have here and there brought about.

Mill's reflections on the possibility of an afterlife are based on his phenomenalism, and similar views have been iterated by several philosophers since—among them, J. M. E. McTaggart and C. J. Ducasse. Phenomenalism is a view according to which all knowledge of fact, including knowledge of physical objects, is derived from the direct awareness of one's own sensations and feelings, which can, accordingly, be considered the primary realities.[4] Now all the putative evidence against the possibility of a life beyond the grave is based, as Mill points out, upon the perishability of material things, and, in particular, of our own bodies. But if material things are, as Mill and others have thought, only inferred things or "permanent possibilities of sensations," and hence have no reality except in reference to our feelings and sensations, then it is plain that no conclusions respecting their perishability can be transferred to that to which they are subordinate—viz., sensations and feelings. There is, therefore, no absurdity in supposing these latter to continue beyond the death of the body. But with his characteristic candor, our author reminds us that this is likewise no positive argument *for* our continued existence beyond death, its whole force being to *remove* what

[4] This important theory of Mill's is developed in *An Examination of Sir William Hamilton's Philosophy* (3rd ed.; London, 1867), ch. 11.

has been thought to be evidence against it. So we are left, as in so many questions of religion, with a total absence of evidence on either side—not merely a lack of evidence sufficient to prove anything, but no evidence at all.[5]

The discussion of revelation is essentially an elaboration upon, and defense of, Hume's famous argument against the credibility of miracles, and, like Hume, Mill does not concern himself with a review of the ostensible evidence for divine interventions in nature, which is fairly familiar, but with the more basic question of what *would* constitute adequate evidence if we should have it. Hume pointed out, in effect,[6] (1) that miracles are by their very nature extraordinary or unusual, (2) that the only evidence we now have for them is the testimony of alleged witnesses, remotely removed from us in time, rather than the evidence of our own experience, and (3) that human beings are, as we do know from our own experience, occasionally dishonest and, when honest, sometimes fallible, credulous, inaccurate, or prone to exaggeration. Hence it follows, Hume said, that no alleged miracle is credible—for in the case of any such, it is always more probable that the testimony is erroneous than that the miracle occurred; or, turning this around, that a miracle occurred is credible *only* if the erroneousness of the testimony for it would be more miraculous or out of keeping with our experience than the miracle itself —a condition which never, by its very nature, obtains. This argument, it should be noted, does not prove that no miracle has ever occurred, but it comes to much the same thing, in purporting to show that belief in any particular miracle, on the basis of testimony, however good, is always irrational.

Hume's argument has been criticized on the ground that it establishes only a negative presumption against divine revela-

_____

[5] The kind of thing which would constitute evidence for survival after death, which some investigators believe we actually possess, would be certain paranormal phenomena such as reports of mediums.

[6] *An Inquiry Concerning Human Understanding,* Section X (Liberal Arts Press edition pp. 117-124).

tions, and that by the same reasoning we are forbidden ever to accept *any* testimony that runs counter to what we have personally observed—the testimony of scientists, for instance, concerning novel discoveries which happen not to have come under our notice.[7] Mill's concern is to show that this presumption, though negative, is a very strong one—similar to the presumption against witchcraft, for instance—and not comparable to the presumption against what is merely novel or unexpected. Most people have never seen a man die in battle, for example, but it is no mark of irrationality to believe testimony, under certain circumstances, that this or that particular man was killed in battle. This, though not a *part* of our personal experience, is nonetheless entirely *in keeping* with our experience—with what we have observed are the effects of severe wounds under other circumstances, with what we may have seen of human combat in other forms, with the ephemeral character of life generally, as we witness it daily, and with the mortality of men in particular, and so on. A miracle, on the other hand, is not merely no part of our experience, but is, by its very nature, something wholly incompatible with our experience; for a miracle, unlike what is merely novel or surprising, is supposed to be *contrary* to the very laws of nature which the whole of our lifetime's experience has tended to confirm as being without exception; otherwise, there would be no point in calling it a miracle. The supposed analogy, then, between the miraculous and the unexpected is so weak as to have no force at all. Nor ought we to say that this answer of Mill's begs the question, in assuming the very thing at issue, viz., that no one has ever witnessed miracles. Mill makes no such assumption. The argument is addressed, as was Hume's, only to those people (by far the greater part of mankind) who have only other people's testimony for the miraculous. It does not pretend to have weight with people who claim to have witnessed supernatural interventions as fairly commonplace occurrences.

[7] See e.g., The Most Rev. M. Sheehan, *Apologetics and Catholic Doctrine* (Dublin, 1954-55), I, 70.

The general tendency of Mill's reflections on religion is, then, skeptical; but it would be wrong to call them one-sided, it being no part of his aim to defend skepticism. But this skepticism, finally, leads him to introduce an idea which was subsequently developed by William James in "The Will to Believe," perhaps the most widely read essay on the rationality of faith ever written in English. James contended that one may reasonably *affirm* certain religious beliefs, under carefully defined circumstances, even when evidence for such beliefs is wholly lacking. Mill goes not nearly so far, insisting always that belief, in so far as it is rational, is proportioned precisely to evidence. We may, however, with no affront to reason, *hope* that the assurances religion offers may be true, and indeed, we *should* hope that they are, hoping that life is not so perishable as it seems, and that divine justice, though there is no sign of it in the world, may nevertheless be real. It may indeed be a mark of foolishness to hope for what is plainly impossible, and somewhat idle to hope for what is evidently improbable, but the whole case is altered when, as in the case of so many religious questions, evidence is lacking to render the thing aspired after either the least bit probable or the least improbable. One may, if one chooses, assume (without reason) that certain religious assurances—a life after death, for instance—are false; but one will need then to be reminded that this assumption *is* arbitrary, being, if Mill is right, something having no evidence for it at all. On the other hand, one may, if one chooses, hope that such assurances are true, and again one can be reminded that this is only a hope, resting on no reason at all. From the standpoint of rationality, the two positions are on a level, being equally lacking in it. But the first sort of attitude has the debilitating effect on one's character and energies that pessimism generally has, while the latter has just the opposite, and is, in fact, the kind of attitude upon which many of the hard-won blessings of life and society have always depended. It may be a kind of folly to go on hoping that one's deepest desires are somehow to be fulfilled, when one has no reason for thinking so—but it is no less a folly to suppose from the start that they will not, and the first kind of foolishness has this advantage, at least, that it tends toward personal happiness and the elevation of life, whereas the second kind tends toward the reverse, and has nothing, not even rationality, in its favor.

This rationalism of Mill's in religious matters is plainly opposed to the much older theological traditions that elevate faith above reason, and nowhere has this opposition been more forcefully and eloquently expressed than by Mill himself, in his now famous criticism of Henry Mansel's theology, a part of which has been added to the present volume as "The Moral Attributes of God."

Mansel's main thesis, defended in his lectures on the *Limits of Religious Thought* (1858), was that God and his ways, though mysterious and in fact incomprehensible to human reason, should and indeed must be devoutly believed in and approved, on faith. Of course theologians have, almost since the beginnings of religious philosophy, felt obliged by the evident disparity between their conceptions of God and their view of his creation, to speak of truths that are above reason, some even maintaining that the mysterious is part of the very essence of religion, but few have gone so far as Mansel in attempting a philosophical proof of this. Both St. Bonaventura and St. Thomas Aquinas fortified this way of thinking by their perfection of the theory of analogical predication, according to which finite men are entitled to assign certain familiar attributes, such as "good" and "wise," to an infinite God, provided it is realized that these expressions cannot then have the same meaning that they have in ordinary discourse nor, indeed, any meaning which the human intellect can really comprehend, and this view, in some version or other, is at least implicit in the thought of most orthodox theologians since then.

Mansel sought to base his thesis upon certain logical and metaphysical principles, borrowed largely from the philosophy of Sir William Hamilton (1788-1856). Hamilton, in opposition to the skepticism of Hume, had argued that belief or trust is prior to knowledge, echoing St. Anselm's *Credo, ut intelligam.* By "knowledge" he meant reasoned conviction; but since the data or principles of reason itself are of necessity *not* based upon reason, they must, he concluded, be not known but rather believed without proof, rendering such belief prior and even superior to knowledge. Moreover, he pointed out, the fact that some proposition expresses what is rationally inconceivable is no sufficient ground for treating it as false, inasmuch as many things now regarded as obviously true, such as physical action at a distance, were once declared to be inconceivable to the very reason that has discovered them. But most important of all, Hamilton, following suggestions in Kant's treatment of the antinomies, invented a principle according to which men are sometimes *obliged* to believe what they cannot know, and what is, in fact, forever rationally inconceivable to them. This principle he called the "Law of the Conditioned," and it was, in part, to the effect that there are many propositions which, together with their denials, formulate what is rationally inconceivable; since, however, (according to this Law) one of any such pair of inconceivables is the contradictory of the other, it follows that one of them must necessarily be true. Examples of such propositions are that space is limited, that it is composed of parts, that time had a beginning or will have an end, that men have free will, and so on, none of which, Hamilton thought, can be conceived as even possible, but none of whose denials is conceivable either, though each such statement or its denial, must, by the logical rule of excluded middle, nevertheless be true.[8]

It was essentially these principles that Mansel applied to

[8] These views of Hamilton's are developed in his *Lectures on Metaphysics,* edited by H. L. Mansel and John Veitch (London and Edinburgh, 1858), especially chs. 9, 11, 39, 40 and Appendix, Part V; his "Philosophy of the Unconditioned," *Edinburgh Review,* Vol. 50 (Oct. 1829), republished in *Discussions in Philosophy, Literature and Education* (Edinburgh, 1852); and his *Dissertations,* appended to his edition of Reid's *Works* (Edinburgh, 1846). They are discussed by Mill in *An Examination of Sir William Hamilton's Philosophy* (3rd ed.; London, 1867), chs. 5 and 6.

religious questions, as Hamilton himself had not done to any
extent. Mansel believed that, by means of them, he could
show that, while an absolute and infinite God cannot be conceived without contradiction, we are nevertheless obliged to
believe in him. The very conception of God, as an absolute,
infinite first cause, involves numberless absurdities, he maintained, but we *know* that many other such apparent absurdities are true nonetheless. Confronted with any doctrine of
theology, therefore, we should give or withhold assent to it
only on the basis of the evidence, or lack of evidence, of its
divine origin, giving no independent consideration at all to
the question whether or not the doctrine in question appears
to us as inconceivable, absurd, or morally perverse. God, for
instance, is conceived as both absolute and as a first cause; but
as absolute, and thus independent of and unrelated to anything else, he cannot really be thought of as the cause of anything, which he nevertheless is. Again, considered as an infinite being, God must be actually everything and potentially
nothing, since any potentiality would impose limitations upon
him; yet he must also, inconsistently with this, be potentially
everything and actually nothing, for if there is anything he
cannot become, he again is a limited being. These and similar
considerations seemed to Mansel to show that the finite understanding of man cannot begin to form a clear conception of
God without falling into contradiction, that the concepts of
human reason are, therefore, forever inadequate for a true
philosophy of religion, and that man must be content with a
docta ignorantia resting entirely on faith and divine revelation.[9]

This philosophy is, of course, not only plainly at odds with
Mill's attitude toward questions of religion, but contrary to
the whole spirit of his philosophy; indeed, for all its ingenuity,
it seemed to him the most morally pernicious doctrine of his
day.[10] That doctrine, it has been noted, was not novel in his
day, and it may be added that, though Mansel himself is now

9 Mill discusses these views in *An Examination of Sir William Hamilton's Philosophy* (3rd ed.; London, 1867), ch. 7.
10 *Ibid.,* p. 109.

largely forgotten, the view he represented by no means faded away after Mill's attack upon it. Indeed, the resurgence of theology in our own time has brought with it new and vociferous champions of what are essentially the same ideas, wherein questions of religion are once and for all severed from those of reason, and the very incomprehensibility of religious doctrines is here and there advocated as a basis for firm conviction in their truth.

RICHARD TAYLOR

NOTE ON THE TEXT

The present edition of Mill's "Theism" is reprinted from the fourth edition of *Three Essays on Religion* (London, 1875). The first edition appeared in 1874, the year after Mill's death. No changes were made in succeeding editions.

In this edition, spelling and punctuation have been carefully modified to conform to present-day American usage. The publisher's editorial staff has added a number of supplementary footnotes, enclosed in brackets, to aid the reader.

The Appendix, "The Moral Attributes of God," is reprinted from the third and last edition of Mill's *An Examination of Sir William Hamilton's Philosophy* (London, 1867). Minor changes in punctuation have been made, and several lengthy footnotes enlarging upon the discussion of Mansel have been omitted.

O.P.

SELECTED BIBLIOGRAPHY

MILL'S MAJOR WORKS

A System of Logic. 2 vols. London, 1843; 8th ed., 1872.

Principles of Political Economy. 2 vols. London, 1848; 7th ed., 1871.

On Liberty. London, 1859.

Dissertations and Discussions. 2 vols. London, 1859; 3 vols., 1867; 4 vols., 1875.

Considerations on Representative Government. London, 1861.

Utilitarianism. London, 1863.

An Examination of Sir William Hamilton's Philosophy. London, 1865; 3rd ed., 1867.

The Subjection of Women. London, 1869.

POSTHUMOUSLY PUBLISHED

Autobiography. Edited by Helen Taylor. London, 1873.

Letters of John Stuart Mill. Edited by Hugh Elliott. 2 vols. London, 1910.

Nature, the Utility of Religion, Theism, Being Three Essays on Religion. London, 1874.

COLLATERAL READING

Anschutz, Richard Paul. *The Philosophy of J. S. Mill.* Oxford, 1953.

Bain, Alexander. *John Stuart Mill: A Criticism; with Personal Recollections.* New York, 1882.

Britton, Karl. *John Stuart Mill.* London, 1953.

Douglas, Charles. *J. S. Mill, A Study of His Philosophy.* Edinburgh, 1895.

Höffding, Harald. *A History of Modern Philosophy,* Vol. II. London, 1900.

Minto, William, and Mitchell, J. M. "Mill," in *Encyclopaedia Britannica,* 11th ed. Edinburgh, 1910.

Packe, Michael St. John. *The Life of John Stuart Mill.* London, 1954.

Stephen, Sir Leslie. *The English Utilitarians,* Vol. III. London, 1900.

THEISM

PART ONE

INTRODUCTION

The contest which subsists from of old between believers and unbelievers in natural and revealed religion has, like other permanent contests, varied materially in its character from age to age, and the present generation, at least in the higher regions of controversy, shows, as compared with the eighteenth and the beginning of the nineteenth century, a marked alteration in the aspect of the dispute. One feature of this change is so apparent as to be generally acknowledged: the more softened temper in which the debate is conducted on the part of unbelievers. The reactionary violence, provoked by the intolerance of the other side, has in a great measure exhausted itself. Experience has abated the ardent hopes once entertained of the regeneration of the human race by merely negative doctrine—by the destruction of superstition. The philosophical study of history, one of the most important creations of recent times, has rendered possible an impartial estimate of the doctrines and institutions of the past, from a relative instead of an absolute point of view—as incidents of human development at which it is useless to grumble, and which may deserve admiration and gratitude for their effects in the past even though they may be thought incapable of rendering similar services to the future. And the position assigned to Christianity or Theism by the more instructed of those who reject the supernatural is that of things once of great value but which can now be done without rather than, as formerly, of things misleading and noxious *ab initio*.

Along with this change in the moral attitude of thoughtful unbelievers toward the religious ideas of mankind a corresponding difference has manifested itself in their intellectual attitude. The war against religious beliefs in the last century was carried on principally on the ground of common sense or of logic; in the present age, on the ground of science. The progress of the physical sciences is considered to have established, by conclusive evidence, matters of fact with which the religious traditions of mankind are not reconcilable, while the science of human nature and history is considered to show that the creeds of the past are natural growths of the human mind in particular stages of its career, destined to disappear and give place to other convictions in a more advanced stage. In the progress of discussion this last class of considerations seems even to be superseding those which address themselves directly to the question of truth. Religions tend to be discussed, at least by those who reject them, less as intrinsically true or false than as products thrown up by certain states of civilization and which, like the animal and vegetable productions of a geological period, perish in those which succeed it from the cessation of the conditions necessary to their continued existence.

This tendency of recent speculation to look upon human opinions pre-eminently from a historical point of view, as facts obeying laws of their own, and requiring, like other observed facts, a historical or a scientific explanation (a tendency not confined to religious subjects), is by no means to be blamed, but to be applauded, not solely as drawing attention to an important and previously neglected aspect of human opinions, but because it has a real though indirect bearing upon the question of their truth. For whatever opinion a person may adopt on any subject that admits of controversy, his assurance if he be a cautious thinker cannot be complete unless he is able to account for the existence of the opposite opinion. To ascribe it to the weakness of the human understanding is an explanation which cannot be sufficient for such a thinker, for he will be slow to assume that he has himself a less share of that infirmity than the rest of mankind, and that error is more likely to be on the other side than on his own. In his examination of evidence the persuasion of others, perhaps of mankind in general, is one of the data of the case, one of the phenomena to be accounted for. As the human intellect, though weak, is not essentially perverted, there is a certain presumption of the truth of any opinion held by many human minds, requiring to be rebutted by assigning some other real or possible cause for its prevalence. And this consideration has a special relevance to the inquiry concerning the foundations of theism, in as much as no argument for the truth of theism is more commonly invoked or more confidently relied on than the general assent of mankind.

But while giving its full value to this historical treatment of the religious question, we ought not therefore to let it supersede the dogmatic. The most important quality of an opinion on any momentous subject is its truth or falsity, which to us resolves itself into the sufficiency of the evidence on which it rests. It is indispensable that the subject of religion should from time to time be reviewed as a strictly scientific question, and that its evidences should be tested by the same scientific methods and on the same principles as those of any of the speculative conclusions drawn by physical science. It being granted then that the legitimate conclusions of science are entitled to prevail over all opinions, however widely held, which conflict with them, and that the canons of scientific evidence which the successes and failures of two thousand years have established are applicable to all subjects on which knowledge is attainable, let us proceed to consider what place there is for religious beliefs on the platform of science, what evidences they can appeal to, such as science can recognize, and what foundation there is for the doctrines of religion considered as scientific theorems.

In this inquiry we of course begin with natural religion, the doctrine of the existence and attributes of God.

THEISM

Though I have defined the problem of natural theology to
be that of the existence of God or of a god rather than of gods,
there is the amplest historical evidence that the belief in gods
is immeasurably more natural to the human mind than the
belief in one author and ruler of nature, and that this more
elevated belief is, compared with the former, an artificial
product, requiring (except when impressed by early education)
a considerable amount of intellectual culture before it can be
reached. For a long time, the supposition appeared forced and
unnatural that the diversity we see in the operations of nature
can all be the work of a single will. To the untaught mind,
and to all minds in prescientific times, the phenomena of
nature seem to be the result of forces altogether heterogene-
ous, each taking its course quite independently of the others;
and though to attribute them to conscious wills is eminently
natural, the natural tendency is to suppose as many such independent wills as there are distinguishable forces of sufficient
importance and interest to have been remarked and named.
There is no tendency in polytheism as such to transform itself
spontaneously into monotheism. It is true that in polytheistic
systems generally the deity whose special attributes inspire the
greatest degree of awe is usually supposed to have a power of
controlling the other deities; and even in the most degraded
perhaps of all such systems, the Hindu, adulation heaps upon
the divinity who is the immediate object of adoration epithets like those habitual to believers in a single god. But there
is no real acknowledgment of one governor. Every god nor-
mally rules his particular department, though there may be a
still stronger god whose power when he chooses to exert it
can frustrate the purposes of the inferior divinity. There could
be no real belief in one creator and governor until mankind
had begun to see in the apparently confused phenomena
which surrounded them a system capable of being viewed as

the possible working out of a single plan. This conception of the world was perhaps anticipated (though less frequently than is often supposed) by individuals of exceptional genius, but it could only become common after a rather long cultivation of scientific thought.

The special mode in which scientific study operates to instill monotheism in place of the more natural polytheism is in no way mysterious. The specific effect of science is to show by accumulating evidence that every event in nature is connected by laws with some fact or facts which preceded it, or, in other words, depends for its existence on some antecedent, but yet not so strictly on one as not to be liable to frustration or modification from others; for these distinct chains of causation are so entangled with one another, the action of each cause is so interfered with by other causes, though each acts according to its own fixed law, that every effect is truly the result rather of the aggregate of all causes in existence than of any one only; and nothing takes place in the world of our experience without spreading a perceptible influence of some sort through a greater or less portion of nature, and making perhaps every portion of it slightly different from what it would have been if that event had not taken place. Now, when once the double conviction has found entry into the mind—that every event depends on antecedents, and at the same time that to bring it about many antecedents must concur, perhaps all the antecedents in nature, in so much that a slight difference in any one of them might have prevented the phenomenon or materially altered its character—the conviction follows that no one event, certainly no one kind of events, can be absolutely preordained or governed by any being but one who holds in his hand the reins of all nature, and not of some department only. At least if a plurality be supposed it is necessary to assume so complete a concert of action and unity of will among them that the difference is for most purposes immaterial between such a theory and that of the absolute unity of the godhead.

The reason, then, why monotheism may be accepted as the

representative of theism in the abstract is not so much because it is the theism of all the more improved portions of the human race, as because it is the only theism which can claim for itself any footing on scientific ground. Every other theory of the government of the universe by supernatural beings is inconsistent either with the carrying on of that government through a continual series of natural antecedents according to fixed laws, or with the interdependence of each of these series upon all the rest, which are the two most general results of science.

Setting out, therefore, from the scientific view of nature as one connected system, or united whole, united not like a web composed of separate threads in passive juxtaposition with one another, but rather like the human or animal frame, an apparatus kept going by perpetual action and reaction among all its parts, it must be acknowledged that the question to which theism is an answer is at least a very natural one and issues from an obvious want of the human mind. Accustomed as we are to find, in proportion to our means of observation, a definite beginning to each individual fact, and since wherever there is a beginning we find that there was an antecedent fact (called by us a cause), a fact but for which the phenomenon which thus commences would not have been, it was impossible that the human mind should not ask itself whether the whole of which these particular phenomena are a part had not also a beginning, and if so, whether that beginning was not an origin; whether there was not something antecedent to the whole series of causes and effects that we term "nature," and but for which nature itself would not have been. From the first recorded speculation this question has never remained without a hypothetical answer. The only answer which has long continued to afford satisfaction is theism.

Looking at the problem, as it is our business to do, merely as a scientific inquiry, it resolves itself into two questions. First, is the theory which refers the origin of all the phenomena of nature to the will of a creator consistent or not with the ascertained results of science? Secondly, assuming it to be consistent, will its proofs bear to be tested by the principles of evidence and canons of belief by which our long experience of scientific inquiry has proved the necessity of being guided?

First, then: There is one conception of theism which is consistent, another which is radically inconsistent, with the most general truths that have been made known to us by scientific investigation.

The one which is inconsistent is the conception of God governing the world by acts of variable will. The one which is consistent is the conception of a God governing the world by invariable laws.

The primitive, and even, in our own day, the vulgar, conception of the divine rule is that the one God, like the many gods of antiquity, carries on the government of the world by special decrees, made *pro hac vice*. Although supposed to be omniscient as well as omnipotent, he is thought not to make up his mind until the moment of action; or at least not so conclusively but that his intentions may be altered up to the very last moment by appropriate solicitation. Without entering into the difficulties of reconciling this view of the divine government with the prescience and the perfect wisdom ascribed to the deity, we may content ourselves with the fact that it contradicts what experience has taught us of the manner in which things actually take place. The phenomena of nature do take place according to general laws. They do originate from definite, natural antecedents. Therefore, if their ultimate origin is derived from a will, that will must have established the general laws and willed the antecedents. If there be a creator, his intention must have been that events should depend upon antecedents and be produced according to fixed laws. But this being conceded, there is nothing in scientific experience inconsistent with the belief that those laws and sequences are themselves due to a divine will. Neither are we obliged to suppose that the divine will exerted itself once for all and, after putting a power into the system which enabled it to go on of itself, has ever since let it alone. Science contains nothing repugnant to the supposition that every event which takes place results from a specific volition of the presiding power provided that this power adheres in its particular volitions to general laws laid down by itself. The common opinion is that this hypothesis tends more to the glory of the deity than the supposition that the universe was made so that it could go on of itself. There have been thinkers however—of no ordinary eminence (of whom Leibniz was one)—who thought the last the only supposition worthy of the deity, and protested against likening God to a clockmaker whose clock will not go unless he puts his hand to the machinery and keeps it going. With such considerations we have no concern in this place. We are looking at the subject not from the point of view of reverence but from that of science, and with science both these suppositions as to the mode of the divine action are equally consistent.

We must now, however, pass to the next question. There is nothing to disprove the creation and government of nature by a sovereign will, but is there anything to prove it? Of what nature are its evidences; and weighed in the scientific balance, what is their value?

THE EVIDENCES OF THEISM

The evidences of a creator are not only of several distinct kinds but of such diverse characters that they are adapted to minds of very different descriptions, and it is hardly possible for any mind to be equally impressed by them all. The familiar classification of them into proofs *a priori* and *a posteriori* marks that, when looked at in a purely scientific view, they belong to different schools of thought. Accordingly, though the unthoughtful believer whose creed really rests on authority gives an equal welcome to all plausible arguments in support of the belief in which he has been brought up, philosophers who have had to make a choice between the *a priori* and the *a posteriori* methods in general science seldom fail, while insisting on one of these modes of support for religion, to speak with more or less of disparagement of the other. It is our duty in the present inquiry to maintain complete impartiality and to give a fair examination to both. At the same time I entertain a strong conviction that one of the two modes of argument is in its nature scientific, the other not only unscientific but condemned by science. The scientific argument is that which reasons from the facts and analogies of human experience as a geologist does when he infers the past states of our terrestrial globe, or an astronomical observer when he draws conclusions respecting the physical composition of the heavenly bodies. This is the *a posteriori* method, the principal application of which to theism is the argument (as it is called) of design. The mode of reasoning which I call unscientific, though in the opinion of some thinkers it is also a legitimate mode of scientific procedure, is that which infers external, objective facts from ideas or convictions of our minds. I say this independently of any opinion of my own respecting the origin of our ideas or convictions; for even if we were unable to point out any manner in which the idea of God, for example, can have grown up from the impressions of experience, still the idea can only prove the idea, and not the objective fact, unless indeed the fact is supposed (agreeably to the Book of Genesis) to have been handed down by tradition from a time when there was direct, personal intercourse with the Divine Being; in which case the argument is no longer *a priori*. The supposition that an idea or a wish or a need, even if native to the mind, proves the reality of a corresponding object derives all its plausibility from the belief already in our minds that we were made by a benignant Being who would not have implanted in us a groundless belief, or a want which he did not afford us the means of satisfying, and is therefore a palpable *petitio principii* if adduced as an argument to support the very belief which it presupposes.

At the same time, it must be admitted that all *a priori* systems, whether in philosophy or religion, do, in some sense, profess to be founded on experience since, though they affirm the possibility of arriving at truths which transcend experience, they yet make the facts of experience their starting point (as what other starting point is possible?). They are entitled to consideration in so far as it can be shown that experience gives any countenance either to them or to their method of inquiry. Professedly *a priori* arguments are not unfrequently of a mixed nature, partaking in some degree of the *a posteriori* character, and may often be said to be *a posteriori* arguments in disguise, the *a priori* considerations acting chiefly in the way of making some particular *a posteriori* argument tell for more than its worth. This is emphatically true of the argument for theism which I shall first examine—the necessity of a First Cause. For this has in truth a wide basis of experience in the universality of the relation of cause and effect among the phenomena of nature, while at the same time theological philosophers have not been content to let it rest upon this basis, but have affirmed causation as a truth of reason apprehended intuitively by its own light.

ARGUMENT FOR A FIRST CAUSE

The argument for a First Cause admits of being, and is, presented as a conclusion from the whole of human experience. Everything that we know (it is argued) had a cause, and owed its existence to that cause. How then can it be but that the world, which is but a name for the aggregate of all that we know, has a cause to which it is indebted for its existence?

The fact of experience, however, when correctly expressed, turns out to be, not that everything which we know derives its existence from a cause, but only every event or change. There is in nature a permanent element, and also a changeable: the changes are always the effects of previous changes;

the permanent existences, so far as we know, are not effects at all. It is true, we are accustomed to say not only of events, but of objects, that they are produced by causes, as water by the union of hydrogen and oxygen. But by this we only mean that when they begin to exist, their beginning is the effect of a cause. But their beginning to exist is not an object, it is an event. If it be objected that the cause of a thing's beginning to exist may be said with propriety to be the cause of the thing itself, I shall not quarrel with the expression. But that which in an object begins to exist is that in it which belongs to the changeable element in nature: the outward form and the properties depending on mechanical or chemical combinations of its component parts. There is in every object another and a permanent element, viz., the specific elementary substance or substances of which it consists and their inherent properties. These are not known to us as beginning to exist: within the range of human knowledge they had no beginning, consequently no cause; though they themselves are causes or concauses of everything that takes place. Experience therefore affords no evidences, not even analogies, to justify our extending to the apparently immutable a generalization grounded only on our observation of the changeable.

As a fact of experience, then, causation cannot legitimately be extended to the material universe itself, but only to its changeable phenomena; of these, indeed, causes may be affirmed without any exception. But what causes? The cause of every change is a prior change, and such it cannot but be; for if there were no new antecedent, there would not be a new consequent. If the state of facts which brings the phenomenon into existence had existed always or for an indefinite duration, the effect also would have existed always or been produced an indefinite time ago. It is thus a necessary part of the fact of causation, within the sphere of our experience, that the causes as well as the effects had a beginning in time, and were themselves caused. It would seem, therefore, that our experience, instead of furnishing an argument for a First Cause, is repugnant to it, and that the very essence of causation as it exists within the limits of our knowledge is incompatible with a First Cause.

But it is necessary to look more particularly into the matter and analyze more closely the nature of the causes of which mankind have experience. For if it should turn out that though all causes have a beginning, there is in all of them a permanent element which had no beginning; this permanent element may with some justice be termed a first or universal cause, in as much as though not sufficient of itself to cause anything, it enters as a concause into all causation. Now it happens that the last result of physical inquiry, derived from the converging evidences of all branches of physical science, does, if it holds good, land us, so far as the material world is concerned, in a result of this sort. Whenever a physical phenomenon is traced to its cause, that cause when analyzed is found to be a certain quantum of force, combined with certain collocations. And the last great generalization of science, the conservation of force, teaches us that the variety in the effects depends partly upon the *amount* of the force, and partly upon the diversity of the collocations. The force itself is essentially one and the same; and there exists of it in nature a fixed quantity, which (if the theory be true) is never increased or diminished. Here then we find, even in the changes of material nature, a permanent element—to all appearance the very one of which we were in quest. This it is apparently to which if to anything we must assign the character of First Cause, the cause of the material universe. For all effects may be traced up to it, while it cannot be traced up, by our experience, to anything beyond; its transformations alone can be so traced, and of them the cause always includes the force itself: the same quantity of force in some previous form. It would seem then that in the only sense in which experience supports in any shape the doctrine of a First Cause, viz., as the primeval and universal element in all causes, the First Cause can be no other than Force.

We are, however, by no means at the end of the question.

On the contrary, the greatest stress of the argument is exactly at the point which we have now reached. For it is maintained that mind is the only possible cause of force; or rather, perhaps, that mind is a force, and that all other force must be derived from it in as much as mind is the only thing which is capable of originating change. This is said to be the lesson of human experience. In the phenomena of inanimate nature the force which works is always a pre-existing force, not originated but transferred. One physical object moves another by giving out to it the force by which it has first been itself moved. The wind communicates to the waves, or to a windmill, or a ship part of the motion which has been given to itself by some other agent. In voluntary action alone we see a commencement, an origination of motion; since all other causes appear incapable of this origination, experience is in favor of the conclusion that all the motion in existence owed its beginning to this one cause: voluntary agency, if not that of man, then of a more powerful Being.

This argument is a very old one. It is to be found in Plato; not, as might have been expected, in the *Phaedo,* where the arguments are not such as would now be deemed of any weight, but in his latest production, the *Leges* [Laws]. And it is still one of the most telling arguments with the more metaphysical class of defenders of natural theology.

Now, in the first place, if there be truth in the doctrine of the conservation of force, in other words, the constancy of the total amount of force in existence, this doctrine does not change from true to false when it reaches the field of voluntary agency. The will does not, any more than other causes, create force: granting that it originates motion, it has no means of doing so but by converting into that particular manifestation a portion of force which already existed in other forms. It is known that the source from which this portion of force is derived is chiefly, or entirely, the force evolved in the processes of chemical composition and decomposition which constitute the body of nutrition: the force so liberated becomes a fund upon which every muscular and even every merely nervous action, as of the brain in thought, is a draft. It is in this sense only that, according to the best lights of science, volition is an originating cause. Volition, therefore, does not answer to the idea of a First Cause; since force must in every instance be assumed as prior to it, and there is not the slightest color, derived from experience, for supposing force itself to have been created by a volition. As far as anything can be concluded from human experience, force has all the attributes of a thing eternal and uncreated.

This, however, does not close the discussion. For though whatever verdict experience can give in the case is against the possibility that will ever originates force, yet if we can be assured that neither does force originate will, will must be held to be an agency, if not prior to force, yet coeternal with it; and if it be true that will can originate, not indeed force but the transformation of force from some other of its manifestations into that of mechanical motion, and that there is within human experience no other agency capable of doing so, the argument for a will as the originator, though not of the universe, yet of the cosmos, or order of the universe, remains unanswered.

But the case thus stated is not conformable to fact. Whatever volition can do in the way of creating motion out of other forms of force, and generally of evolving force from a latent into a visible state, can be done by many other causes. Chemical action, for instance; electricity; heat; the mere presence of a gravitating body—all these are causes of mechanical motion on a far larger scale than any volitions which experience presents to us; and in most of the effects thus produced the motion given by one body to another is not, as in the ordinary cases of mechanical action, motion that has first been given to that other by some third body. The phenomenon is not a mere passing on of mechanical motion, but a creation of it out of a force previously latent or manifesting itself in some other form. Volition, therefore, regarded as an agent in the material universe, has no exclusive privilege of origination: all that it can originate is also originated by other transforming agents. If it be said that those other agents must have had the force they give out put into them from elsewhere, I answer that this is no less true of the force which volition disposes of. We know that this force comes from an external source, the chemical action of the food and air. The force by which the phenomena of the material world are produced circulates through all physical agencies in a never-ending, though sometimes intermitting, stream. I am, of course, speaking of volition only in its action on the material world. We have nothing to do here with the freedom of the will itself as a mental phenomenon—with the *vexata questio* whether volition is self-determining or determined by causes. To the question now on hand it is only the effects of volition that are relevant, not its origin. The assertion is that physical nature must have been produced by a will because nothing but will is known to us as having the power of originating the production of phenomena. We have seen that, on the contrary, all the power that will possesses over phenomena is shared, as far as we have the means of judging, by other and much more powerful agents, and that in the only sense in which those agents do not originate neither does will originate. No prerogative, therefore, can, on the ground of experience, be assigned to volition above other natural agents as a producing cause of phenomena. All that can be affirmed by the strongest assertor of the freedom of the will is that volitions are themselves uncaused and are therefore alone fit to be the First or Universal Cause. But, even assuming volitions to be uncaused, the properties of matter, so far as experience discloses, are uncaused also and have the advantage over any particular volition in being, so far as experience can show, eternal. Theism, therefore, in so far as it rests on the necessity of a First Cause, has no support from experience.

To those who, in default of experience, consider the necessity of a First Cause as a matter of intuition, I would say that it is needless, in this discussion, to contest their premises, since admitting that there is and must be a First Cause it has now been shown that several other agencies than will can lay equal claim to that character. One thing only may be said which requires notice here. Among the facts of the universe to be accounted for, it may be said, is mind; and it is self-evident that nothing can have produced mind but mind.

The special indications that mind is deemed to give, pointing to intelligent contrivance, belong to a different portion of this inquiry. But if the mere existence of mind is supposed to require as a necessary antecedent another mind greater and more powerful, the difficulty is not removed by going one step back: the creating mind stands as much in need of another mind to be the source of its existence as the created mind. Be it remembered that we have no direct knowledge (at least apart from revelation) of a mind which is even apparently eternal, as force and matter are: an eternal mind is, as far as the present argument is concerned, a simple hypothesis to account for the minds which we know to exist. Now it is essential to a hypothesis that if admitted it should at least remove the difficulty and account for the facts. But it does not account for mind to refer one mind to a prior mind for its origin. The problem remains unsolved, the difficulty undiminished, nay, rather increased.

To this it may be objected that the causation of every human mind is matter of fact, since we know that it had a beginning in time. We even know, or have the strongest grounds for believing, that the human species itself had a beginning in time. For there is a vast amount of evidence that the state of our planet was once such as to be incompatible with animal life, and that human life is of very much more modern origin than animal life. In any case, therefore, the fact must be faced that there must have been a cause which called the first human mind, nay the very first germ of organic life, into existence. No such difficulty exists in the supposition of an Eternal Mind. If we did not know that mind on our earth began to exist, we might suppose it to be uncaused; and we may still suppose this of the mind to which we ascribe its existence.

To take this ground is to return into the field of human experience and to become subject to its canons, and we are then entitled to ask where is the proof that nothing can have caused a mind except another mind. From what, except from experience, can we know what can produce what—what causes are adequate to what effects? That nothing can *consciously* produce mind but mind is self-evident, being involved in the meaning of the words; but that there cannot be unconscious production must not be assumed, for it is the very point to be proved. Apart from experience, and arguing on what is called reason, that is, on supposed self-evidence, the notion seems to be that no causes can give rise to products of a more precious or elevated kind than themselves. But this is at variance with the known analogies of nature. How vastly nobler and more precious, for instance, are the higher vegetables and animals than the soil and manure out of which, and by the properties of which, they are raised up! The tendency of all recent speculation is toward the opinion that the development of inferior orders of existence into superior, the substitution of greater elaboration and higher organization for lower, is the general rule of nature. Whether it is so or not, there are at least in nature a multitude of facts bearing that character, and this is sufficient for the argument.

Here, then, this part of the discussion may stop. The result it leads to is that the First-Cause argument is in itself of no value for the establishment of theism, because no cause is needed for the existence of that which has no beginning, and both matter and force (whatever metaphysical theory we may give of the one or the other) have had, so far as our experience can teach us, no beginning—which cannot be said of mind. The phenomena or changes in the universe have indeed each of them a beginning and a cause, but their cause is always a prior change; nor do the analogies of experience give us any reason to expect, from the mere occurrence of changes, that if we could trace back the series far enough we should arrive at a primeval volition. The world does not by its mere existence bear witness to a god: if it gives indications of one, these must be given by the special nature of the phenomena, by what they present that resembles adaptation to an end—of which hereafter. If, in default of evidence from experience, the evidence of intuition is relied upon, it may be answered that if mind, as mind, presents intuitive evidence of having been created, the creative mind must do the same, and we are no nearer to the First Cause than before. But if there be nothing in the nature of mind which in itself implies a creator, the minds which have a beginning in time, as all minds have which are known to our experience, must indeed have been caused, but it is not necessary that their cause should have been a prior intelligence.

ARGUMENT FROM THE GENERAL CONSENT OF MANKIND

Before proceeding to the argument from marks of design, which, as it seems to me, must always be the main strength of natural theism, we may dispose briefly of some other arguments which are of little scientific weight, but which have greater influence on the human mind than much better arguments, because they are appeals to authority, and it is by authority that the opinions of the bulk of mankind are principally and not unnaturally governed. The authority invoked is that of mankind generally, and specially of some of its wisest men; particularly such as were in other respects conspicuous examples of breaking loose from received prejudices. Socrates and Plato, Bacon, Locke, and Newton, Descartes and Leibniz are common examples.

It may doubtless be good advice to persons who in point of knowledge and cultivation are not entitled to think themselves competent judges of difficult questions to bid them content themselves with holding that true which mankind generally believe, and so long as they believe it; or that which has been believed by those who pass for the most eminent among the minds of the past. But to a thinker the argument from other people's opinions has little weight. It is but secondhand evidence and merely admonishes us to look out for and weigh the reasons on which this conviction of mankind or of wise men was founded. Accordingly, those who make any claim to philosophic treatment of the subject employ this general consent chiefly as evidence that there is in the mind of man an intuitive perception, or an instinctive sense, of Deity. From the generality of the belief they infer that it is inherent in our constitution; from which they draw the conclusion, a precarious one indeed, but conformable to the general mode of proceeding of the intuitive philosophy, that the belief must be true; though as applied to theism this argument begs the question, since it has itself nothing to rest upon but the belief that the human mind was made by a God who would not deceive his creatures.

But, indeed, what ground does the general prevalence of the belief in deity afford us for inferring that this belief is native to the human mind, and independent of evidence? Is it then so very devoid of evidence, even apparent? Has it so little semblance of foundation in fact that it can only be accounted for by the supposition of its being innate? We should not expect to find theists believing that the appearances in nature of a contriving Intelligence are not only insufficient but are not even plausible, and cannot be supposed to have carried conviction either to the general or to the wiser mind. If there are external evidences of theism, even if not perfectly conclusive, why need we suppose that the belief of its truth was the result of anything else? The superior minds to whom an appeal is made, from Socrates downward, when they professed to give the grounds of their opinion, did not say that they found the belief in themselves without knowing from whence it came, but ascribed it, if not to revelation, either to some metaphysical argument or to those very external evidences which are the basis of the argument from design.

If it be said that the belief in deity is universal among barbarous tribes and among the ignorant portion of civilized populations, who cannot be supposed to have been impressed

by the marvelous adaptations of nature, most of which are unknown to them, I answer that the ignorant in civilized countries take their opinions from the educated, and that in the
case of savages, if the evidence is insufficient, so is the belief.
The religious belief of savages is not belief in the god of natural theology, but a mere modification of the crude generalization which ascribes life, consciousness, and will to all natural
powers of which they cannot perceive the source or control
the operation. And the divinities believed in are as numerous
as those powers. Each river, fountain, or tree has a divinity of
its own. To see in this blunder of primitive ignorance the
hand of the Supreme Being implanting in his creatures an instinctive knowledge of his existence is a poor compliment to
the Deity. The religion of the savages is fetishism of the gross-
est kind, ascribing animation and will to individual objects,
and seeking to propitiate them by prayer and sacrifice. That
this should be the case is the less surprising when we remember that there is not a definite boundary line broadly separat-
ing the conscious human being from inanimate objects. Between these and man there is an intermediate class of objects,
sometimes much more powerful than man, which do possess
life and will, viz., the brute animals, which in an early stage
of existence play a very great part in human life; making it
the less surprising that the line should not at first be quite
distinguishable between the animate and the inanimate part
of nature. As observation advances, it is perceived that the
majority of outward objects have all their important qualities
in common with entire classes or groups of objects which com-
port themselves exactly alike in the same circumstances, and
in these cases the worship of visible objects is exchanged for
that of an invisible Being supposed to preside over the whole
class. This step in generalization is slowly made, with hesitation and even terror, as we still see in the case of ignorant
populations, with what difficulty experience disabuses them of
belief in the supernatural powers and terrible resentment of a
particular idol. Chiefly by these terrors the religious impressions of barbarians are kept alive, with only slight modifica-

tions, until the theism of cultivated minds is ready to take their place. And the theism of cultivated minds, if we take their own word for it, is always a conclusion either from arguments called rational or from the appearances in nature.

It is needless here to dwell upon the difficulty of the hypothesis of a natural belief not common to all human beings, an instinct not universal. It is conceivable, doubtless, that some men might be born without a particular natural faculty, as some are born without a particular sense. But when this is the case we ought to be much more particular as to the proof that it really is a natural faculty. If it were not a matter of observation but of speculation that men can see, if they had no apparent organ of sight, and no perceptions or knowledge but such as they might conceivably have acquired by some circuitous process through their other senses, the fact that men exist who do not even suppose themselves to see would be a considerable argument against the theory of a visual sense. But it would carry us too far to press, for the purposes of this discussion, an argument which applies so largely to the whole of the intuitional philosophy. The strongest Intuitionist will not maintain that a belief should be held for instinctive when evidence (real or apparent) sufficient to engender it is universally admitted to exist. To the force of the evidence must be, in this case, added all the emotional or moral causes which incline men to the belief, the satisfaction which it gives to the obstinate questionings with which men torment themselves respecting the past, the hopes which it opens for the future, the fears also, since fear as well as hope predisposes to belief, and to these in the case of the more active spirits must always have been added a perception of the power which belief in the supernatural affords for governing mankind either for their own good, or for the selfish purposes of the governors.

The general consent of mankind does not, therefore, afford ground for admitting, even as a hypothesis, the origin in an inherent law of the human mind of a fact otherwise so more than sufficiently, so amply, accounted for.

THE ARGUMENT FROM CONSCIOUSNESS

There have been numerous arguments, indeed almost every religious metaphysician has one of his own, to prove the existence and attributes of God from what are called truths of reason, supposed to be independent of experience. Descartes, who is the real founder of the intuitional metaphysics, draws the conclusion immediately from the first premise of his philosophy, the celebrated assumption that whatever he could very clearly and distinctly apprehend must be true. The idea of a God, perfect in power, wisdom, and goodness, is a clear and distinct idea and must therefore, on this principle, correspond to a real object. This bold generalization, however, that a conception of the human mind proves its own objective reality, Descartes is obliged to limit by the qualification—"if the idea includes existence." Now the idea of God implying the union of all perfections, and existence being a perfection, the idea of God proves his existence. This very simple argument, which denies to man one of his most familiar and most precious attributes, that of idealizing, as it is called—of constructing from the materials of experience a conception more perfect than experience itself affords—is not likely to satisfy anyone in the present day. More elaborate, though scarcely more successful, efforts have been made by many of Descartes' successors to derive knowledge of the Deity from an inward light: to make it a truth not dependent on external evidence, a fact of direct perception or, as they are accustomed to call it, of consciousness. The philosophical world is familiar with the attempt of Cousin [1] to make out that whenever we perceive a particular object, we perceive along with it, or are conscious of, God; and also with the celebrated refutation of this doctrine by Sir William Hamilton. [2] It would be waste of time to

[1] [Victor Cousin (1792-1867). French philosopher. He was the first to formulate eclecticism as a method.]

[2] [Sir William Hamilton (1788-1856). Scottish philosopher, professor of logic and metaphysics. Among his published works are *Metaphysics* and

examine any of these theories in detail. While each has its own particular logical fallacies, they labor under the common infirmity that one man cannot, by proclaiming with ever so much confidence that *he* perceives an object, convince other people that they see it, too. If, indeed, he laid claim to a divine faculty of vision, vouchsafed to him alone, and making him cognizant of things which men not thus assisted have not the capacity to see, the case might be different. Men have been able to get such claims admitted, and other people can only require of them to show their credentials. But when no claim is set up to any peculiar gift but we are told that all of us are as capable as the prophet of seeing what he sees, feeling what he feels, nay, that we actually do so, and when the utmost effort of which we are capable fails to make us aware of what we are told we perceive, this supposed universal faculty of intuition is but

> The dark lantern of the Spirit
> Which none see by but those who bear it;

and the bearers may fairly be asked to consider whether it is not more likely that they are mistaken as to the origin of an impression in their minds than that others are ignorant of the very existence of an impression in theirs.

The inconclusiveness, in a speculative point of view, of all arguments from the subjective notion of Deity to its objective reality was well seen by Kant, the most discriminating of the *a priori* metaphysicians, who always kept the two questions— the origin and composition of our ideas, and the reality of the corresponding objects—perfectly distinct. According to Kant the idea of the Deity is native to the mind, in the sense that it is constructed by the mind's own laws and not derived from without; but this idea of speculative reason cannot be shown by any logical process or perceived by direct apprehension to have a corresponding reality outside the human mind. To

---

Logic, published posthumously 1858-1860. For a critical analysis of Hamilton's philosophy see Mill's *An Examination of Sir William Hamilton's Philosophy*, 3rd ed., 1867.]

Kant, God is neither an object of direct consciousness nor a conclusion of reasoning, but a necessary assumption—necessary, not by a logical, but a practical necessity, imposed by the reality of the moral law. Deity is a fact of consciousness: "thou shalt" is a command issuing from the recesses of our being, and not to be accounted for by any impressions derived from experience; and this command requires a commander, though it is not perfectly clear whether Kant's meaning is that conviction of a law includes conviction of a lawgiver, or only that a Being of whose will the law is an expression is eminently desirable. If the former be intended, the argument is founded on a double meaning of the word "law." A rule to which we feel it a duty to conform has in common with laws commonly so called the fact of claiming our obedience, but it does not follow that the rule must originate, like the laws of the land, in the will of a legislator or legislators external to the mind. We may even say that a feeling of obligation which is merely the result of a command is not what is meant by moral obligation, which, on the contrary, supposes something that the internal conscience bears witness to as binding in its own nature, and which God, in superadding his command, conforms to and perhaps declares, but does not create. Conceding, then, for the sake of the argument, that the moral sentiment is as purely of the mind's own growth, the obligation of duty as entirely independent of experience and acquired impressions, as Kant or any other metaphysician ever contended, it may yet be maintained that this feeling of obligation rather excludes than compels the belief in a divine legislator merely as the source of the obligation; and, as a matter of fact, the obligation of duty is both theoretically acknowledged and practically felt in the fullest manner by many who have no positive belief in God, though seldom, probably, without habitual and familiar reference to him as an ideal conception. But if the existence of God as a wise and just lawgiver is not a necessary part of the feelings of morality, it may still be maintained that those feelings make his existence eminently desirable. No doubt, they do, and that is the great rea-

son why we find that good men and women cling to the belief and are pained by its being questioned. But surely it is
not legitimate to assume that in the order of the universe
whatever is desirable is true. Optimism, even when a God is
already believed in, is a thorny doctrine to maintain, and had
to be taken by Leibniz in the limited sense that the universe,
being made by a good being, is the best universe possible—
not the best absolutely: that the divine power, in short, was
not equal to making it more free from imperfections than it
is. But optimism prior to belief in a God, and as the ground
of that belief, seems one of the oddest of all speculative delusions. Nothing, however, I believe, contributes more to keep
up the belief in the general mind of humanity than this feeling of its desirableness, which, when clothed, as it very often
is, in the forms of an argument, is a naive expression of the
tendency of the human mind to believe what is agreeable to
it. Positive value the argument, of course, has none.

Without dwelling further on these or on any other of the
a priori arguments for theism, we will no longer delay passing to the far more important argument of the appearances of
contrivance in nature.

THE ARGUMENT FROM MARKS OF DESIGN IN NATURE

We now at last reach an argument of a really scientific character, which does not shrink from scientific tests, but claims
to be judged by the established canons of induction. The design argument is wholly grounded on experience. Certain
qualities, it is alleged, are found to be characteristic of such
things as are made by an intelligent mind for a purpose. The
order of nature, or some considerable parts of it, exhibit these
qualities in a remarkable degree. We are entitled, from this
great similarity in the effects, to infer similarity in the cause,

and to believe that things which it is beyond the power of man to make, but which resemble the works of man in all but power, must also have been made by Intelligence armed with a power greater than human.

I have stated this argument in its fullest strength, as it is stated by its most thoroughgoing assertors. A very little consideration, however, suffices to show that though it has some force, its force is very generally overrated. Paley's illustration of a watch puts the case much too strongly.[1] If I found a watch on an apparently desolate island, I should, indeed, infer that it had been left there by a human being; but the inference would not be from marks of design, but because I already knew by direct experience that watches are made by men. I should draw the inference no less confidently from a footprint or from any relic, however insignificant, which experience has taught me to attribute to man: as geologists infer the past existence of animals from coprolites, though no one sees marks of design in a coprolite. The evidence of design in creation can never reach the height of direct induction; it amounts only to the inferior kind of inductive evidence called analogy. Analogy agrees with induction in this, that they both argue that a thing known to resemble another in certain circumstances (call those circumstances A and B) will resemble it in another circumstance (call it C). But the difference is that in induction A and B are known, by a previous comparison of many instances, to be the very circumstances on which C depends or with which it is in some way connected. When this has not been ascertained, the argument amounts only to this, that since it is not known with which of the circumstances existing in the known case C is connected, they may as well be A and B as any others; and therefore there is a greater probability of C in cases where we know that A and B exist than in cases of which we know nothing at all. This argument is of a weight very difficult to estimate at all, and impossible to

---

1 [William Paley (1743-1805). English theologian and Utilitarian philosopher. He is the author of *The Principles of Morals and Political Philosophy* (1785), *Horae Paulinae* (1790), and *Natural Theology* (1802).]

estimate precisely. It may be very strong when the known points of agreement, *A* and *B,* etc., are numerous and the known points of difference few, or very weak when the reverse is the case; but it can never be equal in validity to a real induction. The resemblances between some of the arrangements in nature and some of those made by man are considerable, and even as mere resemblances afford a certain presumption of similarity of cause, but how great that presumption is it is hard to say. All that can be said with certainty is that these likenesses make creation by intelligence considerably more probable than if the likenesses had been less, or than if there had been no likeness at all.

This mode, however, of stating the case does not do full justice to the evidence of theism. The design argument is not drawn from mere resemblances in nature to the works of human intelligence, but from the special character of those resemblances. The circumstances in which it is alleged that the world resembles the works of man are not circumstances taken at random, but are particular instances of a circumstance which experience shows to have a real connection with an intelligent origin—the fact of conspiring to an end. The argument therefore is not one of mere analogy. As mere analogy it has its weight, but it is more than analogy. It surpasses analogy exactly as induction surpasses it. It is an inductive argument.

This, I think, is undeniable, and it remains to test the argument by the logical principles applicable to induction. For this purpose it will be convenient to handle, not the argument as a whole, but some one of the most impressive cases of it, such as the structure of the eye or of the ear. It is maintained that the structure of the eye proves a designing mind. To what class of inductive arguments does this belong, and what is its degree of force?

The species of inductive arguments are four in number, corresponding to the four inductive methods: the methods of agreement, of difference, of residues, and of concomitant variations. The argument under consideration falls within the first of these divisions, the method of agreement. This is, for reasons known to inductive logicians, the weakest of the four, but the particular argument is a strong one of the kind. It may be logically analyzed as follows:

The parts of which the eye is composed, and the collocations which constitute the arrangement of those parts, resemble one another in this very remarkable property, that they all conduce to enabling the animal to see. These things being as they are, the animal sees: if any one of them were different from what it is, the animal, for the most part, would either not see or would not see equally well. And this is the only marked resemblance that we can trace among the different parts of this structure beyond the general likeness of composition and organization which exists among all other parts of the animal. Now the particular combination of organic elements called an eye had, in every instance, a beginning in time and must therefore have been brought together by a cause or causes. The number of instances is immeasurably greater than is, by the principles of inductive logic, required for the exclusion of a random concurrence of independent causes; or, speaking technically, for the elimination of chance. We are therefore warranted by the canons of induction in concluding that what brought all these elements together was some cause common to them all; and in as much as the elements agree in the single circumstance of conspiring to produce sight there must be some connection by way of causation between the cause which brought those elements together, and the fact of sight.

This I conceive to be a legitimate inductive inference, and the sum and substance of what induction can do for theism. The natural sequel of the argument would be this: Sight, being a fact not precedent but subsequent to the putting together of the organic structure of the eye, can only be connected with the production of that structure in the character of a final, not an efficient, cause; that is, it is not sight itself but an antecedent idea of it that must be the efficient cause. But this at once marks the origin as proceeding from an intelligent will.

I regret to say, however, that this latter half of the argument is not so inexpugnable as the former half. Creative fore-

thought is not absolutely the only link by which the origin of
the wonderful mechanism of the eye may be connected with
the fact of sight. There is another connecting link on which
attention has been greatly fixed by recent speculations, and
the reality of which cannot be called in question, though its
adequacy to account for such truly admirable combinations as
some of those in nature is still and will probably long remain
problematical. This is the principle of "the survival of the
fittest."

This principle does not pretend to account for the commencement of sensation or of animal or vegetable life. But
assuming the existence of some one or more very low forms of
organic life in which there are no complex adaptations nor
any marked appearances of contrivance, and supposing, as experience warrants us in doing, that many small variations from
those simple types would be thrown out in all directions,
which would be transmissible by inheritance, and of which
some would be advantageous to the creature in its struggle for
existence and others disadvantageous, the forms which are
advantageous would always tend to survive and those which
are disadvantageous to perish. And thus there would be a
constant though slow general improvement of the type as it
branched out into many different varieties, adapting it to
different media and modes of existence until it might possibly, in countless ages, attain to the most advanced examples
which now exist.

It must be acknowledged that there is something very star-
tling, and *prima facie* improbable in this hypothetical history
of nature. It would require us, for example, to suppose that
the primeval animal of whatever nature it may have been
could not see and had at most such slight preparation for seeing as might be constituted by some chemical action of light
upon its cellular structure. One of the accidental variations
which are liable to take place in all organic beings would at
some time or other produce a variety that could see in some
imperfect manner, and this peculiarity being transmitted by
inheritance, while other variations continued to take place in

other directions, a number of races would be produced who, by the power of even imperfect sight, would have a great advantage over all other creatures which could not see and would in time extirpate them from all places, except, perhaps, a few very peculiar situations underground. Fresh variations supervening would give rise to races with better and better seeing powers until we might at last reach as extraordinary a combination of structures and functions as are seen in the eye of man and of the more important animals. Of this theory when pushed to this extreme point, all that can now be said is that it is not so absurd as it looks, and that the analogies which have been discovered in experience, favorable to its possibility, far exceed what anyone could have supposed beforehand. Whether it will ever be possible to say more than this is at present uncertain. The theory if admitted would be in no way whatever inconsistent with creation. But it must be acknowledged that it would greatly attenuate the evidence for it.

Leaving this remarkable speculation to whatever fate the progress of discovery may have in store for it, I think it must be allowed that in the present state of our knowledge the adaptations in nature afford a large balance of probability in favor of creation by intelligence. It is equally certain that this is no more than a probability, and that the various other arguments of natural theology which we have considered add nothing to its force. Whatever ground there is, revelation apart, to believe in an Author of Nature is derived from the appearances in the universe. Their mere resemblance to the works of man, or to what man could do if he had the same power over the materials of organized bodies which he has over the materials of a watch, is of some value as an argument of analogy: but the argument is greatly strengthened by the properly inductive considerations which establish that there is some connection through causation between the origin of the arrangements of nature and the ends they fulfill—an argument which is in many cases slight, but in others, and chiefly in the nice and intricate combinations of vegetable and animal life, is of considerable strength.

PART TWO

ATTRIBUTES

The question of the existence of a Deity, in its purely scientific aspect, standing as is shown in the First Part, it is next to be considered, given the indications of a Deity, what *sort* of a Deity do they point to? What attributes are we warranted, by the evidence which nature affords of a creative mind, in assigning to that mind?

It needs no showing that the power, if not the intelligence, must be so far superior to that of man as to surpass all human estimate. But from this to omnipotence and omniscience there is a wide interval. And the distinction is of immense practical importance.

It is not too much to say that every indication of design in the cosmos is so much evidence against the omnipotence of the designer. For what is meant by design? Contrivance: the adaptation of means to an end. But the necessity for contrivance—the need of employing means—is a consequence of the limitation of power. Who would have recourse to means if to attain his end his mere word was sufficient? The very idea of means implies that the means have an efficacy which the direct action of the being who employs them has not. Otherwise they are not means but an encumbrance. A man does not use machinery to move his arms. If he did, it could only be when paralysis had deprived him of the power of moving them by volition. But if the employment of contrivance is in itself a sign of limited power, how much more so is the careful and skillful choice of contrivances? Can any wisdom be shown in the selection of means when the means have no efficacy but what is given them by the will of him who employs them, and when his will could have bestowed the same efficacy on any other means? Wisdom and contrivance are shown in overcoming

33

difficulties, and there is no room for them in a being for whom no difficulties exist. The evidences, therefore, of natural theology distinctly imply that the author of the cosmos worked under limitations; that he was obliged to adapt himself to conditions independent of his will and to attain his ends by such arrangements as those conditions admitted of.

And this hypothesis agrees with what we have seen to be the tendency of the evidences in another respect. We found that the appearances in nature point indeed to an origin of the cosmos or order in nature, and indicate that origin to be design, but do not point to any commencement, still less creation, of the two great elements of the universe, the passive element and the active element, matter and force. There is in nature no reason whatever to suppose that either matter or force, or any of their properties, were made by the being who was the author of the collocations by which the world is adapted to what we consider as its purposes; or that he has power to alter any of those properties. It is only when we consent to entertain this negative supposition that there arises a need for wisdom and contrivance in the order of the universe. The Deity had on this hypothesis to work out his ends by combining materials of a given nature and properties. Out of these materials he had to construct a world in which his designs should be carried into effect through given properties of matter and force, working together and fitting into one another. This did require skill and contrivance, and the means by which it is effected are often such as justly excite our wonder and admiration; but exactly because it requires wisdom, it implies limitation of power, or rather the two phrases express different sides of the same fact.

If it be said that an Omnipotent Creator, though under no necessity of employing contrivances such as man must use, thought fit to do so in order to leave traces by which man might recognize his creative hand, the answer is that this equally supposes a limit to his omnipotence. For if it was his will that men should know that they themselves and the world are his work, he, being omnipotent, had only to will that they should be aware of it. Ingenious men have sought for reasons why God might choose to leave his existence so far a matter of doubt that men should not be under an absolute necessity of knowing it, as they are of knowing that three and two make five. These imagined reasons are very unfortunate specimens of casuistry; but even did we admit their validity, they are of no avail on the supposition of omnipotence, since if it did not please God to implant in man a complete conviction of his existence, nothing hindered him from making the conviction fall short of completeness by any margin he chose to leave. It is usual to dispose of arguments of this description by the easy answer that we do not know what wise reasons the Omniscient may have had for leaving undone things which he had the power to do. It is not perceived that this plea itself implies a limit to omnipotence. When a thing is obviously good and obviously in accordance with what all the evidences of creation imply to have been the Creator's design, and we say we do not know what good reason he may have had for not doing it, we mean that we do not know to what other, still better object—to what object still more completely in the line of his purposes, he may have seen fit to postpone it. But the necessity of postponing one thing to another belongs only to limited power. Omnipotence could have made the objects compatible. Omnipotence does not need to weigh one consideration against another. If the Creator, like a human ruler, had to adapt himself to a set of conditions which he did not make, it is as unphilosophical as presumptuous in us to call him to account for any imperfections in his work, to complain that he left anything in it contrary to what, if the indications of design prove anything, he must have intended. He must at least know more than we know, and we cannot judge what greater good would have had to be sacrificed or what greater evil incurred if he had decided to remove this particular blot. Not so if he be omnipotent. If he be that, he must himself have willed that the two desirable objects should be incompatible; he must himself have willed that the obstacle to his supposed design should be insuperable. It cannot therefore *be* his design. It will not do to say that it was, but that he had other designs which interfered with it; for no one purpose imposes necessary limitations on another in the case of a Being not restricted by conditions of possibility.

Omnipotence, therefore, cannot be predicated of the Creator on grounds of natural theology. The fundamental principles of natural religion as deduced from the facts of the universe negative his omnipotence. They do not, in the same manner, exclude omniscience: if we suppose limitation of power, there is nothing to contradict the supposition of perfect knowledge and absolute wisdom. But neither is there anything to prove it. The knowledge of the powers and properties of things necessary for planning and executing the arrangements of the cosmos is no doubt as much in excess of human knowledge as the power implied in creation is in excess of human power. And the skill, the subtlety of contrivance, the ingenuity as it would be called in the case of a human work, is often marvelous. But nothing obliges us to suppose that either the knowledge or the skill is infinite. We are not even compelled to suppose that the contrivances were always the best possible. If we venture to judge them as we judge the works of human artificers, we find abundant defects. The human body, for example, is one of the most striking instances of artful and ingenious contrivance which nature offers, but we may well ask whether so complicated a machine could not have been made to last longer and not to get so easily and frequently out of order. We may ask why the human race should have been so constituted as to grovel in wretchedness and degradation for countless ages before a small portion of it was enabled to lift itself into the very imperfect state of intelligence, goodness, and happiness which we enjoy. The divine power may not have been equal to doing more; the obstacles to a better arrangement of things may have been insuperable. But it is also possible that they were not. The skill of the *demiourgos* was sufficient to produce what we see; but we cannot tell that this skill reached the extreme limit of perfection compatible with the material it employed and the forces it had to work with. I know not how we can even satisfy ourselves on grounds of natural theology that the Creator foresees all the future, that he foreknows all the effects that will issue from his own contrivances. There may be great wisdom without the power of foreseeing and calculating everything; and human workmanship teaches us the possibility that the workman's knowledge of the properties of the things he works on may enable him to make arrangements admirably fitted to produce a given result, while he may have very little power of foreseeing the agencies of another kind which may modify or counteract the operation of the machinery he has made. Perhaps a knowledge of the laws of nature on which organic life depends, not much more perfect than the knowledge which man even now possesses of some other natural laws, would enable man, if he had the same power over the materials and the forces concerned which he has over some of those of inanimate nature, to create organized beings not less wonderful nor less adapted to their conditions of existence than those in nature.

Assuming then that while we confine ourselves to natural religion we must rest content with a Creator less than almighty; the question presents itself, of what nature is the limitation of his power? Does the obstacle at which the power of the Creator stops, which says to it: "Thus far shalt thou go and no further," lie in the power of other intelligent beings, or in the insufficiency and refractoriness of the materials of the universe, or must we resign ourselves to admitting the hypothesis that the author of the cosmos, though wise and knowing, was not all-wise and all-knowing, and may not always have done the best that was possible under the conditions of the problem?

The first of these suppositions has until a very recent period been, and in many quarters still is, the prevalent theory even of Christianity. Though attributing, and in a certain sense sincerely, omnipotence to the Creator, the received religion represents him as for some inscrutable reason tolerating the perpetual counteraction of his purposes by the will of another being of opposite character and of great, though inferior, power, the Devil. The only difference on this matter between popular Christianity and the religion of Ormuzd and Ahriman [1] is that the former pays its good Creator the bad compliment of having been the maker of the Devil and of being at all times able to crush and annihilate him and his evil deeds and counsels, which nevertheless he does not do. But, as I have already remarked, all forms of polytheism, and this among the rest, are with difficulty reconcilable with a universe governed by general laws. Obedience to law is the note of a settled government and not of a conflict always going on. When powers are at war with one another for the rule of the world, the boundary between them is not fixed but constantly fluctuating. This may seem to be the case on our planet as between the powers of good and evil when we look only at the results; but when we consider the inner springs we find that both the good and the evil take place in the common course of nature, by virtue of the same general laws originally impressed—the same machinery turning out now good, now evil things, and oftener still, the two combined. The division of power is only apparently variable, but really so regular that, were we speaking of human potentates, we should declare without hesitation that the share of each must have been fixed by previous consent. Upon that supposition, indeed, the result of the combination of antagonist forces might be much the same as on that of a single creator with divided purposes.

But when we come to consider, not what hypothesis may be conceived and possibly reconciled with known facts, but what supposition is pointed to by the evidences of natural religion, the case is different. The indications of design point strongly in one direction—the preservation of the creatures in whose structure the indications are found. Along with the preserving agencies there are destroying agencies which we might be tempted to ascribe to the will of a different creator; but there

[1] [Mill here emphasizes the point that in Zoroastrianism, contrary to the Christian belief, the good spirit (Ormuzd) and the evil (Ahriman) are coeval. They are constantly at war against each other in their effort to influence the conduct of men.]

are rarely appearances of the recondite contrivance of means of destruction except when the destruction of one creature is the means of preservation to others. Nor can it be supposed that the preserving agencies are wielded by one being, the destroying agencies by another. The destroying agencies are a necessary part of the preserving agencies: the chemical compositions by which life is carried on could not take place without a parallel series of decompositions. The great agent of decay in both organic and inorganic substances is oxidation, and it is only by oxidation that life is continued for even the length of a minute. The imperfections in the attainment of the purposes which the appearances indicate have not the air of having been designed. They are like the unintended results of accidents insufficiently guarded against, or of a little excess or deficiency in the quantity of some of the agencies by which the good purpose is carried on, or else they are consequences of the wearing out of a machinery not made to last forever: they point either to shortcomings in the workmanship as regards its intended purpose, or to external forces not under the control of the workman, but which forces bear no mark of being wielded and aimed by any other and rival intelligence. We may conclude, then, that there is no ground in natural theology for attributing intelligence or personality to the obstacles which partially thwart what seem the purposes of the Creator. The limitation of his power more probably results either from the qualities of the material—the substances and forces of which the universe is composed not admitting of any arrangements by which his purposes could be more completely fulfilled; or else, the purposes might have been more fully attained, but the Creator did not know how to do it; creative skill, wonderful as it is, was not sufficiently perfect to accomplish his purposes more thoroughly.

We now pass to the moral attributes of the Deity, so far as indicated in the creation; or (stating the problem in the broadest manner) to the question, what indications nature gives of the purposes of its author. This question bears a very different aspect to us from what it bears to those teachers of natural theology who are encumbered with the necessity of admitting the omnipotence of the Creator. We have not to attempt the impossible problem of reconciling infinite benevolence and justice with infinite power in the Creator of such a world as this. The attempt to do so not only involves absolute contradiction in an intellectual point of view but exhibits to excess the revolting spectacle of a jesuitical defense of moral enormities.

On this topic I need not add to the illustrations given of this portion of the subject in my Essay on Nature.[2] At the stage which our argument has reached there is none of this moral perplexity. Grant that creative power was limited by conditions the nature and extent of which are wholly unknown to us, and the goodness and justice of the Creator may be all that the most pious believe; and all in the work that conflicts with those moral attributes may be the fault of the conditions which left to the Creator only a choice of evils.

It is, however, one question whether any given conclusion is consistent with known facts, and another whether there is evidence to prove it; and if we have no means for judging of the design but from the work actually produced, it is a somewhat hazardous speculation to suppose that the work designed was of a different quality from the result realized. Still, though the ground is unsafe we may, with due caution, journey a certain distance on it. Some parts of the order of nature give much more indication of contrivance than others; many, it is not too much to say, give no sign of it at all. The signs of contrivance are most conspicuous in the structure and processes of vegetable and animal life. But for these, it is probable that the appearances in nature would never have seemed to the thinking part of mankind to afford any proofs of a God. But when a God had been inferred from the organization of living beings, other parts of nature, such as the structure of the solar system, seemed to afford evidences, more or less

_____

[2] [Reference is to the first of the *Three Essays on Religion*, of which the present is the third, and "Utility of Religion" the second.]

strong, in confirmation of the belief; granting, then, a design in nature, we can best hope to be enlightened as to what that design was by examining it in the parts of nature in which its traces are the most conspicuous.

To what purpose, then, do the expedients in the construction of animals and vegetables, which excite the admiration of naturalists, appear to tend? There is no blinking the fact that they tend principally to no more exalted object than to make the structure remain in life and in working order for a certain time: the individual for a few years, the species or race for a longer but still a limited period. And the similar, though less conspicuous, marks of creation which are recognized in inorganic nature are generally of the same character. The adaptations, for instance, which appear in the solar system consist in placing it under conditions which enable the mutual action of its parts to maintain, instead of destroying, its stability, and even that only for a time, vast indeed if measured against our short span of animated existence, but which can be perceived even by us to be limited; for even the feeble means which we possess of exploring the past are believed by those who have examined the subject by the most recent lights to yield evidence that the solar system was once a vast sphere of nebula or vapor and is going through a process which in the course of ages will reduce it to a single and not very large mass of solid matter frozen up with more than arctic cold. If the machinery of the system is adapted to keep itself at work only for a time, still less perfect is the adaptation of it for the abode of living beings, since it is only adapted to them during the relatively short portion of its total duration which intervenes between the time when each planet was too hot and the time when it became or will become too cold to admit of life under the only conditions in which we have experience of its possibility. Or we should perhaps reverse the statement and say that organization and life are only adapted to the conditions of the solar system during a relatively short portion of the system's existence.

The greater part, therefore, of the design of which there is indication in nature, however wonderful its mechanism, is no evidence of any moral attributes, because the end to which it is directed, and its adaptation to which end is the evidence of its being directed to an end at all, is not a moral end: it is not the good of any sentient creature, it is but the qualified permanence, for a limited period, of the work itself, whether animate or inanimate. The only inference that can be drawn from most of it respecting the character of the Creator is that he does not wish his works to perish as soon as created; he wills them to have a certain duration. From this alone nothing can be justly inferred as to the manner in which he is affected toward his animate or rational creatures.

After deduction of the great number of adaptations which have no apparent object but to keep the machine going, there remain a certain number of provisions for giving pleasure to living beings, and a certain number of provisions for giving them pain. There is no positive certainty that the whole of these ought not to take their place among the contrivances for keeping the creature or its species in existence; for both the pleasures and the pains have a conservative tendency; the pleasures being generally so disposed as to attract to the things which maintain individual or collective existence, the pains so as to deter from such as would destroy it.

When all these things are considered it is evident that a vast deduction must be made from the evidences of a Creator before they can be counted as evidences of a benevolent purpose—so vast indeed that some may doubt whether after such a deduction there remains any balance. Yet endeavoring to look at the question without partiality or prejudice and without allowing wishes to have any influence over judgment, it does appear that granting the existence of design, there is a preponderance of evidence that the Creator desired the pleasure of his creatures. This is indicated by the fact that pleasure of one description or another is afforded by almost everything, the mere play of the faculties, physical and mental, being a never-ending source of pleasure, and even painful things giving pleasure by the satisfaction of curiosity and the agreeable sense of acquiring knowledge; and also that pleasure, when experienced, seems to result from the normal working of the machinery, while pain usually arises from some external interference with it and resembles in each particular case the result of an accident. Even in cases when pain results, like pleasure, from the machinery itself, the appearances do not indicate that contrivance was brought into play purposely to produce pain: what is indicated is rather a clumsiness in the contrivance employed for some other purpose. The author of the machinery is no doubt accountable for having made it susceptible to pain; but this may have been a necessary condition of its susceptibility to pleasure; a supposition which avails nothing on the theory of an omnipotent Creator but is an extremely probable one in the case of a contriver working under the limitation of inexorable laws and indestructible properties of matter. The susceptibility being conceded as a thing which did enter into design, the pain itself usually seems like a thing undesigned; a casual result of the collision of the organism with some outward force to which it was not intended to be exposed, and which, in many cases, provision is even made to hinder it from being exposed to. There is, therefore, much appearance that pleasure is agreeable to the Creator, while there is very little, if any, appearance that pain is so: and there is a certain amount of justification for inferring, on grounds of natural theology alone, that benevolence is one of the attributes of the Creator. But to jump from this to the inference that his sole or chief purposes are those of benevolence, and that the single end and aim of Creation was the happiness of his creatures, is not only not justified by any evidence but is a conclusion in opposition to such evidence as we have. If the motive of the Deity for creating sentient beings was the happiness of the beings he created, his purpose, in our corner of the universe at least, must be pronounced, taking past ages and all countries and races into account, to have been thus far an ignominious failure; and if God had no purpose but our happiness and that of other living creatures it is not credible that he would have called them into existence with the prospect of being so completely baffled. If man had not the power by the exercise of his own energies for the improvement both of himself and of his outward circumstances to do for himself and other creatures vastly more than God had in the first instance done, the Being who called him into existence would deserve something very different from thanks at his hands. Of course it may be said that this very capacity of improving himself and the world was given to him by God, and that the change which he will be thereby enabled ultimately to effect in human existence will be worth purchasing by the sufferings and wasted lives of entire geological periods. This may be so; but to suppose that God could not have given him these blessings at a less frightful cost is to make a very strange supposition concerning the Deity. It is to suppose that God could not, in the first instance, create anything better than a Bosjesman or an Andaman Islander,[3] or something still lower, and yet was able to endow the Bosjesman or the Andaman Islander with the power of raising himself into a Newton or a Fénelon.[4] We certainly do not know the nature of the barriers which limit the divine omnipotence; but it is a very odd notion of them that they enable the Deity to confer on an almost bestial creature the power of producing by a succession of efforts what God himself had no other means of creating.

Such are the indications of natural religion in respect to the divine benevolence. If we look for any other of the moral attributes which a certain class of philosophers are accustomed to distinguish from benevolence, as, for example, justice, we find a total blank. There is no evidence whatever in nature for divine justice, whatever standard of justice our ethical opinions may lead us to recognize. There is no shadow of justice in the general arrangements of nature; and what im-

[3] [Both the Bosjesmen and the Andaman Islanders are Indian tribes known for their backward state of civilization.]

[4] [François de Salignac de La Mothe Fénelon (1651-1715). French prelate and writer. Consecrated archbishop of Cambrai 1695. His major works are *Fables*, *Dialogues des mortes*, and *Télémaque*.]

perfect realization it obtains in any human society (a most imperfect realization as yet) is the work of man himself, struggling upward against immense natural difficulties into civilization, and making to himself a second nature, far better and more unselfish than he was created with. But on this point enough has been said in another Essay, already referred to: on Nature.

These, then, are the net results of natural theology on the question of the divine attributes. A being of great but limited power, how or by what limited we cannot even conjecture; of great, and perhaps unlimited, intelligence, but perhaps also more narrowly limited than his power; who desires and pays some regard to the happiness of his creatures, but who seems to have other motives of action which he cares more for, and who can hardly be supposed to have created the universe for that purpose alone. Such is the Deity whom natural religion points to; and any idea of God more captivating than this comes only from human wishes or from the teaching of either real or imaginary revelation.

We shall next examine whether the light of nature gives any indications concerning the immortality of the soul and a future life.

PART THREE

IMMORTALITY

The indications of immortality may be considered in two divisions: those which are independent of any theory respecting the Creator and his intentions, and those which depend upon an antecedent belief on that subject.

Of the former class of arguments speculative men have in different ages put forward a considerable variety, of which those in the *Phaedon* of Plato are an example; but they are for the most part such as have no adherents and need not be seriously refuted now. They are generally founded upon preconceived theories as to the nature of the thinking principle in man, considered as distinct and separable from the body, and on other preconceived theories respecting death. As, for example, that death or dissolution is always a separation of parts; and the soul being without parts, being simple and indivisible, is not susceptible of this separation. Curiously enough, one of the interlocutors in the *Phaedon* anticipates the answer by which an objector of the present day would meet this argument: namely, that thought and consciousness, though mentally distinguishable from the body, may not be a substance separable from it, but a result of it; standing in a relation to it (the illustration is Plato's) like that of a tune to the musical instrument on which it is played, and that the arguments used to prove that the soul does not die with the body would equally prove that the tune does not die with the instrument but survives its destruction and continues to exist apart. In fact, those moderns who dispute the evidences of the immortality of the soul do not, in general, believe the soul to be a substance *per se,* but regard it as the name of a bundle of attributes—the attributes of feeling, thinking, reasoning, believing, willing, etc.; and these attributes they regard as a consequence of the bodily organization, which therefore, they argue, it is as unreasonable to suppose surviving when that organization is dispersed as to suppose the color or odor of a rose surviving when the rose itself has perished. Those, therefore, who would deduce the immortality of the soul from its own nature have first to prove that the attributes in question are not attributes of the body but of a separate substance. Now what is the verdict of science on this point? It is not perfectly conclusive either way. In the first place, it does not prove, experimentally, that any mode of organization has the power of producing feeling or thought. To make that proof good it would be necessary that we should be able to produce an organism, and try whether it would feel; which we cannot do; organisms cannot by any human means be produced, they can only be developed out of a previous organism. On the other hand, the evidence is well nigh complete that all thought and feeling has some action of the bodily organism for its immediate antecedent or accompaniment; that the specific variations and especially the different degrees of complication of the nervous and cerebral organization correspond to differences in the development of the mental faculties; and though we have no evidence, except negative, that the mental consciousness ceases forever when the functions of the brain are at an end, we do know that diseases of the brain disturb the mental functions and that decay or weakness of the brain enfeebles them. We have therefore sufficient evidence that cerebral action is, if not the cause, at least, in our present state of existence, a condition *sine qua non* of mental operations; and that assuming the mind to be a distinct substance, its separation from the body would not be, as some have vainly flattered themselves, a liberation from trammels and restoration to freedom, but would simply put a stop to its functions and remand it to unconsciousness unless and until some other set of conditions supervenes, capable of recalling it into activity, but of the existence of which experience does not give us the smallest indication.

At the same time it is of importance to remark that these

considerations only amount to defect of evidence; they afford
no positive argument against immortality. We must beware of
giving *a priori* validity to the conclusions of an *a posteriori*
philosophy. The root of all *a priori* thinking is the tendency
to transfer to outward things a strong association between the
corresponding ideas in our own minds; and the thinkers who
most sincerely attempt to limit their beliefs by experience,
and honestly believe that they do so, are not always sufficiently
on their guard against this mistake. There are thinkers who
regard it as a truth of reason that miracles are impossible; and
in like manner there are others who, because the phenomena
of life and consciousness are associated in their minds by undeviating experience with the action of material organs, think
it an absurdity *per se* to imagine it possible that those phenomena can exist under any other conditions. But they should
remember that the uniform coexistence of one fact with
another does not make the one fact a part of the other, or the
same with it. The relation of thought to a material brain is
no metaphysical necessity, but simply a constant coexistence
within the limits of observation. And when analyzed to the
bottom on the principles of the associative psychology, the
brain just as much as the mental functions is, like matter itself, merely a set of human sensations either actual or inferred as possible, namely, those which the anatomist has when
he opens the skull, and impressions which we suppose we
should receive of molecular or some other movements when
the cerebral action was going on if there were no bony en-
velope and our senses or our instruments were sufficiently
delicate. Experience furnishes us with no example of any
series of states of consciousness without this group of contingent sensations attached to it; but it is as easy to imagine
such a series of states without, as with, this accompaniment,
and we know of no reason in the nature of things against the
possibility of its being thus disjoined. We may suppose that
the same thoughts, emotions, volitions, and even sensations
which we have here may persist or recommence somewhere
else under other conditions, just as we may suppose that other

thoughts and sensations may exist under other conditions in other parts of the universe. And in entertaining this supposition we need not be embarrassed by any metaphysical difficulties about a thinking substance. Substance is but a general name for the perdurability of attributes: wherever there is a series of thoughts connected together by memories, that constitutes a thinking substance. This absolute distinction in thought and separability in representation of our states of consciousness from the set of conditions with which they are united only by constancy of concomitance is equivalent in a practical point of view to the old distinction of the two substances—matter and mind.

There is, therefore, in science no evidence against the immortality of the soul but that negative evidence which consists in the absence of evidence in its favor. And even the negative evidence is not so strong as negative evidence often is. In the case of witchcraft, for instance, the fact that there is no proof which will stand examination of its having ever existed is as conclusive as the most positive evidence of its nonexistence would be; for it exists, if it does exist, on this earth, where if it had existed the evidence of fact would certainly have been available to prove it. But it is not so as to the soul's existence after death. That it does not remain on earth and go about visibly or interfere in the events of life is proved by the same weight of evidence which disproves witchcraft. But that it does not exist elsewhere, there is absolutely no proof. A very faint, if any, presumption is all that is afforded by its disappearance from the surface of this planet.

Some may think that there is an additional and very strong presumption against the immortality of the thinking and conscious principle from the analysis of all the other objects of nature. All things in nature perish, the most beautiful and perfect being, as philosophers and poets alike complain, the most perishable. A flower of the most exquisite form and coloring grows up from a root, comes to perfection in weeks or months, and lasts only a few hours or days. Why should it be otherwise with man? Why indeed? But why, also, should it *not* be otherwise? Feeling and thought are not merely different from what we call inanimate matter, but are at the opposite pole of existence, and analogical inference has little or no validity from the one to the other. Feeling and thought are much more real than anything else; they are the only things which we directly know to be real, all things else being merely the unknown conditions on which these, in our present state of existence or in some other, depend. All matter apart from the feelings of sentient beings has but a hypothetical and unsubstantial existence; it is a mere assumption to account for our sensations; itself we do not perceive, we are not conscious of it, but only of the sensations which we are said to receive from it: in reality it is a mere name for our expectation of sensations or for our belief that we can have certain sensations when certain other sensations give indication of them. Because these contingent possibilities of sensation sooner or later come to an end and give place to others, is it implied in this, that the series of our feelings must itself be broken off? This would not be to reason from one kind of substantive reality to another, but to draw from something which has no reality except in reference to something else, conclusions applicable to that which is the only substantive reality. Mind (or whatever name we give to what is implied in consciousness of a continued series of feelings) is in a philosophical point of view the only reality of which we have any evidence, and no analogy can be recognized or comparison made between it and other realities because there are no other known realities to compare it with. That is quite consistent with its being perishable; but the question whether it is so or not is *res integra*, untouched by any of the results of human knowledge and experience. The case is one of those very rare cases in which there is really a total absence of evidence on either side, and in which the absence of evidence for the affirmative does not, as in so many cases it does, create a strong presumption in favor of the negative.

The belief, however, in human immortality, in the minds of mankind generally, is probably not grounded on any scientific arguments either physical or metaphysical, but on foundations with most minds much stronger, namely, on one hand, the disagreeableness of giving up existence (to those at least to whom it has hitherto been pleasant), and, on the other hand, the general traditions of mankind. The natural tendency of belief to follow these two inducements—our own wishes and the general assent of other people—has been in this instance reinforced by the utmost exertion of the power of public and private teaching; rulers and instructors having at all times, with the view of giving greater effect to their mandates, whether from selfish or from public motives, encouraged to the utmost of their power the belief that there is a life after death in which pleasures and sufferings far greater than on earth depend on our doing or leaving undone while alive what we are commanded to do in the name of the unseen powers. As causes of belief these various circumstances are most powerful. As rational grounds of it they carry no weight at all.

That what is called the consoling nature of an opinion—that is, the pleasure we should have in believing it to be true—can be a ground for believing it, is a doctrine irrational in itself and which would sanction half the mischievous illusions recorded in history or which mislead individual life. It is sometimes, in the case now under consideration, wrapped up in a quasi-scientific language. We are told that the desire of immortality is one of our instincts, and that there is no instinct which has not corresponding to it a real object fitted to satisfy it. Where there is hunger there is somewhere food, where there is a sexual feeling there is somewhere sex, where there is love there is somewhere something to be loved, and so forth: in like manner, since there is the instinctive desire of eternal life, eternal life there must be. The answer to this is patent on the very surface of the subject. It is unnecessary to go into any recondite considerations concerning instincts, or to discuss whether the desire in question is an instinct or not. Granting that wherever there is an instinct there exists something such as that instinct demands, can it be affirmed that this something exists in boundless quantity or sufficient to satisfy the infinite craving of human desires? What is called the desire of eternal life is simply the desire of life; and does there not exist that which this desire calls for? Is there not life? And is not the instinct, if it be an instinct, gratified by the possession and preservation of life? To suppose that the desire of life guarantees to us personally the reality of life through all eternity is like supposing that the desire of food assures us that we shall always have as much as we can eat through our whole lives and as much longer as we can conceive our lives to be protracted to.

The argument from tradition or the general belief of the human race, if we accept it as a guide to our own belief, must be accepted entire: if so, we are bound to believe that the souls of human beings not only survive after death but show themselves as ghosts to the living; for we find no people who have had the one belief without the other. Indeed it is probable that the former belief originated in the latter, and that primitive men would never have supposed that the soul did not die with the body if they had not fancied that it visited them after death. Nothing could be more natural than such a fancy; it is, in appearance, completely realized in dreams, which in Homer and in all ages like Homer's are supposed to be real apparitions. To dreams we have to add not merely waking hallucinations, but the delusions, however baseless, of sight and hearing, or rather the misinterpretations of those senses: sight or hearing supplying mere hints from which imagination paints a complete picture and invests it with reality. These delusions are not to be judged of by a modern standard; in early times the line between imagination and perception was by no means clearly defined; there was little or none of the knowledge we now possess of the actual course of nature, which makes us distrust or disbelieve any appearance which is at variance with known laws. In the ignorance of men as to what were the limits of nature and what was or was not compatible with it, no one thing seemed, as far as physical considerations went, to be much more improbable than another. In rejecting, therefore, as we do, and as we have the best reason to do, the tales and legends of the actual appearance of disembodied spirits, we take from under the general belief of mankind in a life after death what in all probability was its chief ground and support and deprive it of even the very little value which the opinion of rude ages can ever have as evidence of truth. If it be said that this belief has maintained itself in ages which have ceased to be rude and which reject the superstitions with which it once was accompanied, the same may be said of many other opinions of rude ages, and especially on the most important and interesting subjects, because it is on those subjects that the reigning opinion, whatever it may be, is the most sedulously inculcated upon all who are born into the world. This particular opinion, moreover, if it has on the whole kept its ground, has done so with a constantly increasing number of dissentients, and those especially among cultivated minds. Finally, those cultivated minds which adhere to the belief ground it, we may reasonably suppose, not on the belief of others, but on arguments and evidences; and those arguments and evidences, therefore, are what it concerns us to estimate and judge.

The preceding are a sufficient sample of the arguments for a future life which do not suppose an antecedent belief in the existence, or any theory respecting the attributes of the godhead. It remains to consider what arguments are supplied by such lights, or such grounds of conjecture, as natural theology affords on those great questions.

We have seen that these lights are but faint; that of the existence of a Creator they afford no more than a preponderance of probability; of his benevolence a considerably less preponderance; that there is, however, some reason to think that he cares for the pleasures of his creatures, but by no means that this is his sole care, or that other purposes do not often take precedence of it. His intelligence must be adequate to the contrivances apparent in the universe, but need not be more than adequate to them, and his power is not only not proved to be infinite, but the only real evidences in natural theology tend to show that it is limited, contrivance being a mode of overcoming difficulties, and always supposing difficulties to be overcome.

We have now to consider what inference can legitimately be drawn from these premises in favor of a future life. It seems to me, apart from express revelation, none at all.

The common arguments are: the goodness of God; the improbability that he would ordain the annihilation of his noblest and richest work after the greater part of its few years of life had been spent in the acquisition of faculties which time is not allowed him to turn to fruit; and the special improbability that he would have implanted in us an instinctive desire of eternal life and doomed that desire to complete disappointment.

These might be arguments in a world the constitution of which made it possible without contradiction to hold it for the work of a Being at once omnipotent and benevolent. But they are not arguments in a world like that in which we live. The benevolence of the divine Being may be perfect, but his power being subject to unknown limitations, we know not that he could have given us what we so confidently assert that he must have given—*could* (that is) without sacrificing something more important. Even his benevolence, however justly inferred, is by no means indicated as the interpretation of his whole purpose, and since we cannot tell how far other purposes may have interfered with the exercise of his benevolence, we know not that he *would*, even if he could have granted us eternal life. With regard to the supposed improbability of his having given the wish without its gratification, the same answer may be made; the scheme which either limitation of power or conflict of purposes compelled him to adopt may have *required* that we should have the wish although it were not destined to be gratified. One thing, however, is quite certain in respect to God's government of the world: that he either could not, or would not, grant to us everything we wish. We wish for life, and he has granted some life; that we wish (or some of us wish) for a boundless extent of life and that it is not granted is no exception to the ordinary modes of his government. Many a man would like to be a Croesus or an Augustus Caesar, but has his wishes gratified only to the moderate extent of a pound a week or the secretaryship of his trades union. There is, therefore, no assurance whatever of a life after death on grounds of natural religion. But to anyone who feels it conducive either to his satisfaction or to his usefulness to hope for a future state as a possibility, there is no hindrance to his indulging that hope. Appearances point to the existence of a Being who has great power over us—all the power implied in the creation of the cosmos, or of its organized beings at least—and of whose goodness we have evidence though not of its being his predominant attribute; and as we do not know the limits either of his power or of his goodness, there is room to hope that both the one and the other may extend to granting us this gift provided that it would really be beneficial to us. The same ground which permits the hope warrants us in expecting that if there be a future life it will be at least as good as the present, and will not be wanting in the best feature of the present life—improvability by our own efforts. Nothing can be more opposed to every estimate we can form of probability than the common idea of the future life as a state of rewards and punishments in any other sense than that the consequences of our actions upon our own character and susceptibilities will follow us in the future as they have done in the past and present. Whatever be the probabilities *of* a future life, all the probabilities *in case of* a future life are that such as we have been made or have made ourselves before the change, such we shall enter into the life hereafter; and that the fact of death will make no sudden break in our spiritual life, nor influence our character any otherwise than as any important change in our mode of existence may always be expected to modify it. Our thinking principle has its laws which in this life are invariable, and any analogies drawn from this life must assume that the same laws will continue. To imagine that a miracle will be wrought at death by the act of God making perfect everyone whom it is his will to include among his elect, might be justified by an express revelation duly authenticated, but is utterly opposed to every presumption that can be deduced from the light of nature.

PART FOUR

REVELATION

The discussion in the preceding pages respecting the evidences of theism has been strictly confined to those which are derived from the light of nature. It is a different question what addition has been made to those evidences and to what extent the conclusions obtainable from them have been amplified or modified by the establishment of a direct communication with the Supreme Being. It would be beyond the purpose of this essay to take into consideration the positive evidences of the Christian, or any other, belief which claims to be a revelation from heaven. But such general considerations as are applicable not to a particular system but to revelation generally may properly find a place here and are indeed necessary to give a sufficiently practical bearing to the results of the preceding investigation.

In the first place, then, the indications of a Creator and of his attributes which we have been able to find in nature, though so much slighter and less conclusive even as to his existence than the pious mind would wish to consider them, and still more unsatisfactory in the information they afford as to his attributes, are yet sufficient to give to the supposition of a revelation a standing point which it would not otherwise have had. The alleged revelation is not obliged to build up its case from the foundation; it has not to prove the very existence of the Being from whom it professes to come. It claims to be a message from a Being whose existence, whose power, and, to a certain extent, whose wisdom and goodness are, if not proved, at least indicated with more or less of probability by the phenomena of nature. The sender of the alleged message is not a sheer invention; there are grounds independent of the message itself for belief in his reality; grounds which,

though insufficient for proof, are sufficient to take away all
antecedent improbability from the supposition that a message
may really have been received from him. It is, moreover,
much to the purpose to take notice that the very imperfection
of the evidences which natural theology can produce of the
divine attributes removes some of the chief stumbling blocks
to the belief of a revelation, since the objections grounded on
imperfections in the revelation itself, however conclusive
against it if it is considered as a record of the acts or an expression of the wisdom of a Being of infinite power combined
with infinite wisdom and goodness, are no reason whatever
against its having come from a Being such as the course of nature points to, whose wisdom is possibly, his power certainly,
limited, and whose goodness, though real, is not likely to have
been the only motive which actuated him in the work of creation. The argument of Butler's *Analogy* [1] is, from its own
point of view, conclusive: the Christian religion is open to no
objections, either moral or intellectual, which do not apply at
least equally to the common theory of deism; the morality of
the Gospels is far higher and better than that which shows itself in the order of nature; and what is morally objectionable
in the Christian theory of the world is objectionable only
when taken in conjunction with the doctrine of an omnipotent God, and (at least as understood by the most enlightened
Christians) by no means imports any moral obliquity in a
Being whose power is supposed to be restricted by real, though
unknown, obstacles which prevented him from fully carrying
out his design. The grave error of Butler was that he shrank
from admitting the hypothesis of limited powers, and his appeal consequently amounts to this: the belief of Christians is
neither more absurd nor more immoral than the belief of

[1] [Joseph Butler (1692-1752). English divine and bishop of Durham. Although raised in the deistical tradition at the Presbyterian academy, he
later joined the Church of England and attacked the prevailing deistical
speculations in his *The Analogy* (1733). At Rolls Chapel (1718-26) he
preached his famous sermons, known as the *Fifteen Sermons* (published
1726). Five of the sermons have been reprinted in the "Library of Liberal Arts" under the title *Five Sermons* (LLA 21).]

deists who acknowledge an omnipotent Creator; let us, therefore, in spite of the absurdity and immorality, believe both.
He ought to have said, let us cut down our belief of either to
what does not involve absurdity or immorality, to what is
neither intellectually self-contradictory nor morally perverted.

To return, however, to the main subject: on the hypothesis
of a God who made the world, and in making it had regard,
however that regard may have been limited by other considerations, to the happiness of his sentient creatures, there is no
antecedent improbability in the supposition that his concern
for their good would continue and that he might once or oftener give proof of it by communicating to them some knowledge of himself beyond what they were able to make out by
their unassisted faculties, and some knowledge or precepts use-
ful for guiding them through the difficulties of life. Neither
on the only tenable hypothesis, that of limited power, is it
open to us to object that these helps ought to have been
greater or in any way other than they are. The only question
to be entertained, and which we cannot dispense ourselves
from entertaining, is that of evidence. Can any evidence suf-
fice to prove a divine revelation? And of what nature and
what amount must that evidence be? Whether the special evidences of Christianity or of any other alleged revelation do or
do not come up to the mark is a different question, into which
I do not propose directly to enter. The question I intend to
consider is what evidence is required; what general conditions
it ought to satisfy; and whether they are such as, according to
the known constitution of things, *can* be satisfied.

The evidences of revelation are commonly distinguished as
external or internal. External evidences are the testimony of
the senses or of witnesses. By the internal evidences are meant
the indications which the revelation itself is thought to furnish of its divine origin; indications supposed to consist chiefly
in the excellence of its precepts, and its general suitability to
the circumstances and needs of human nature.

The consideration of these internal evidences is very important, but their importance is principally negative; they may

be conclusive grounds for rejecting a revelation but cannot of themselves warrant the acceptance of it as divine. If the moral character of the doctrines of an alleged revelation is bad and perverting, we ought to reject it from whomsoever it comes, for it cannot come from a good and wise Being. But the excellence of their morality can never entitle us to ascribe to them a supernatural origin, for we cannot have conclusive reason for believing that the human faculties were incompetent to find out moral doctrines of which the human faculties can perceive and recognize the excellence. A revelation, therefore, cannot be proved divine unless by external evidence, that is, by the exhibition of supernatural facts. And we have to consider whether it is possible to prove supernatural facts and, if it is, what evidence is required to prove them.

This question has only, so far as I know, been seriously raised on the skeptical side, by Hume.[2] It is the question involved in his famous argument against miracles: an argument which goes down to the depths of the subject, but the exact scope and effect of which (perhaps not conceived with perfect correctness by that great thinker himself) have in general been utterly misconceived by those who have attempted to answer him. Dr. Campbell,[3] for example, one of the acutest of his antagonists, has thought himself obliged, in order to support the credibility of miracles, to lay down doctrines which virtually go the length of maintaining that antecedent improbability is never a sufficient ground for refusing credence to a statement, if it is well attested. Dr. Campbell's fallacy lay in overlooking a double meaning of the word "improbability," as I have pointed out in my *Logic* and, still earlier, in an editorial note to Bentham's treatise on Evidence.[4]

Taking the question from the very beginning: it is evidently

2 [Cf. Hume's *Inquiry Concerning Human Understanding*, "Library of Liberal Arts" edition (LLA 49), pp. 117-124.

3 [George Campbell (1719-1796). Scottish theologian. Author of *Dissertation on Miracles* (1762) and of *Philosophy of Rhetoric* (1776).]

4 [John Stuart Mill, *A System of Logic*. 2 vols., London, 1843. 8th ed., 1872.]

impossible to maintain that if a supernatural fact really occurs, proof of its occurrence cannot be accessible to the human faculties. The evidence of our senses could prove this as it can prove other things. To put the most extreme case: suppose that I actually saw and heard a Being, either of the human form or of some form previously unknown to me, commanding a world to exist, and a new world actually starting into existence and commencing a movement through space at his command. There can be no doubt that this evidence would convert the creation of worlds from a speculation into a fact of experience. It may be said I could not know that so singular an appearance was anything more than a hallucination of my senses. True; but the same doubt exists at first respecting every unsuspected and surprising fact which comes to light in our physical researches. That our senses have been deceived is a possibility which has to be met and dealt with, and we do deal with it by several means. If we repeat the experiment, and again with the same result, if at the time of the observation the impressions of our senses are in all other respects the same as usual, rendering the supposition of their being morbidly affected in this one particular extremely improbable—above all, if other people's senses confirm the testimony of our own—we conclude, with reason, that we may trust our senses. Indeed, our senses are all that we have to trust to. We depend on them for the ultimate premises even of our reasonings. There is no other appeal against their decision than an appeal from the senses without precautions to the senses with all due precautions. When the evidence on which an opinion rests is equal to that upon which the whole conduct and safety of our lives is founded, we need ask no further. Objections which apply equally to all evidence are valid against none. They only prove abstract fallibility.

But the evidence of miracles, at least to Protestant Christians, is not in our own day of this cogent description. It is not the evidence of our senses, but of witnesses, and even this not at first hand, but resting on the attestation of books and traditions. And even in the case of the original eyewitnesses, the supernatural facts asserted on their alleged testimony are not of the transcendent character supposed in our example, about the nature of which, or the impossibility of their having had a natural origin, there could be little room for doubt. On the contrary, the recorded miracles are, in the first place, generally such as it would have been extremely difficult to verify as matters of fact, and, in the next place, are hardly ever beyond the possibility of having been brought about by human means or by the spontaneous agencies of nature. It is to cases of this kind that Hume's argument against the credibility of miracles was meant to apply.

His argument is: The evidence of miracles consists of testimony. The ground of our reliance on testimony is our experience that, certain conditions being supposed, testimony is generally veracious. But the same experience tells us that even under the best conditions testimony is frequently, either intentionally or unintentionally, false. When, therefore, the fact to which testimony is produced is one the happening of which would be more at variance with experience than the falsehood of testimony, we ought not to believe it. And this rule all prudent persons observe in the conduct of life. Those who do not are sure to suffer for their credulity.[5]

Now a miracle (the argument goes on to say) is in the highest possible degree contradictory to experience; for if it were not contradictory to experience it would not be a miracle. The very reason for its being regarded as a miracle is that it is a breach of a law of nature, that is, of an otherwise invariable and inviolable uniformity in the succession of natural events. There is, therefore, the very strongest reason for disbelieving it that experience can give for disbelieving anything. But the mendacity or error of witnesses, even though numerous and of fair character, is quite within the bounds of even common experience. That supposition, therefore, ought to be preferred.

There are two apparently weak points in this argument. One is that the evidence of experience to which its appeal is made is only negative evidence, which is not so conclusive as

5 [Cf. Hume, op. cit., pp. 123-124.]

positive, since facts of which there had been no previous experience are often discovered and proved by positive experience to be true. The other seemingly vulnerable point is this: The argument has the appearance of assuming that the testimony of experience against miracles is undeviating and indubitable, as it would be if the whole question was about the probability of future miracles, none having taken place in the past; whereas the very thing asserted on the other side is that there have been miracles, and that the testimony of experience is not wholly on the negative side. All the evidence alleged in favor of any miracle ought to be reckoned as counter-evidence in refutation of the ground on which it is asserted that miracles ought to be disbelieved. The question can only be stated fairly as depending on a balance of evidence: a certain amount of positive evidence in favor of miracles, and a negative presumption from the general course of human experience against them.

In order to support the argument under this double correction, it has to be shown that the negative presumption against a miracle is very much stronger than that against a merely new and surprising fact. This, however, is evidently the case. A new physical discovery, even if it consists in the defeating of a well-established law of nature, is but the discovery of another law previously unknown. There is nothing in this but what is familiar to our experience: we were aware that we did not know all the laws of nature, and we were aware that one such law is liable to be counteracted by others. The new phenomenon, when brought to light, is found still to depend on law; it is always exactly reproduced when the same circumstances are repeated. Its occurrence, therefore, is within the limits of variation in experience which experience itself discloses. But a miracle, in the very fact of being a miracle, declares itself to be a supersession not of one natural law by another, but of the law which includes all others, which experience shows to be universal for all phenomena, viz., that they depend on some law, that they are always the same when there are the same phenomenal antecedents, and neither take place in the absence of their phenomenal causes, nor ever fail to take place when the phenomenal conditions are all present.

It is evident that this argument against belief in miracles had very little to rest upon until a comparatively modern stage in the progress of science. A few generations ago the universal dependence of phenomena on invariable laws was not only not recognized by mankind in general, but could not be regarded by the instructed as a scientifically established truth. There were many phenomena which seemed quite irregular in their course, without dependence on any known antecedents; and though, no doubt, a certain regularity in the occurrence of the most familiar phenomena must always have been recognized, yet even in these, the exceptions which were constantly occurring had not yet, by an investigation and generalization of the circumstances of their occurrence, been reconciled with the general rule. The heavenly bodies were from of old the most conspicuous types of regular and unvarying order; yet even among them comets were a phenomenon apparently originating without any law, and eclipses one which seemed to take place in violation of law. Accordingly, both comets and eclipses long continued to be regarded as of a miraculous nature, intended as signs and omens of human fortunes. It would have been impossible in those days to prove to anyone that this supposition was antecedently improbable. It seemed more conformable to appearances than the hypothesis of an unknown law.

Now, however, when in the progress of science all phenomena have been shown by indisputable evidence to be amenable to law, and even in the cases in which those laws have not yet been exactly ascertained, delay in ascertaining them is fully accounted for by the special difficulties of the subject; the defenders of miracles have adapted their argument to this altered state of things by maintaining that a miracle need not necessarily be a violation of law. It may, they say, take place in fulfillment of a more recondite law to us unknown.

If by this it be only meant that the Divine Being, in the exercise of his power of interfering with and suspending his own laws, guides himself by some general principle or rule of action, this, of course, cannot be disproved and is in itself the most probable supposition. But if the argument means that a miracle may be the fulfillment of a law in the same sense in which the ordinary events of nature are fulfillments of laws, it seems to indicate an imperfect conception of what is meant by a law and of what constitutes a miracle.

When we say that an ordinary physical fact always takes place according to some invariable law, we mean that it is connected by uniform sequence or coexistence with some definite set of physical antecedents—that whenever that set is exactly reproduced, the same phenomenon will take place unless counteracted by the similar laws of some other physical antecedents; and that whenever it does take place, it would always be found that its special set of antecedents (or one of its sets if it has more than one) has pre-existed. Now, an event which takes place in this manner is not a miracle. To make it a miracle it must be produced by a direct volition without the use of means, or at least of any means which, if simply repeated, would produce it. To constitute a miracle a phenomenon must take place without having been preceded by any antecedent phenomenal conditions sufficient again to reproduce it, or a phenomenon for the production of which the antecedent conditions existed must be arrested or prevented without the intervention of any phenomenal antecedents which would arrest or prevent it in a future case. The test of a miracle is: were there present in the case such external conditions, such "second causes" we may call them, that whenever these conditions or causes reappear the event will be reproduced? If there were, it is not a miracle; if there were not, it is a miracle, but it is not according to law; it is an event produced without or in spite of law.

It will perhaps be said that a miracle does not necessarily exclude the intervention of second causes. If it were the will of God to raise a thunderstorm by miracle, he might do it by means of winds and clouds. Undoubtedly, but the winds and clouds were either sufficient, when produced, to excite the thunderstorm without other divine assistance, or they were not. If they were not, the storm is not a fulfillment of law, but a violation of it. If they were sufficient, there is a miracle; but it is not the storm; it is the production of the winds and clouds, or whatever link in the chain of causation it was at which the influence of physical antecedents was dispensed with. If that influence was never dispensed with, but the event called miraculous was produced by natural means, and those again by others, and so on from the beginning of things—if the event is no otherwise the act of God than in having been foreseen and ordained by him as the consequence of the forces put in action at the creation—then there is no miracle at all, nor anything different from the ordinary working of God's providence.

For another example: a person professing to be divinely commissioned cures a sick person by some apparently insignificant, external application. Would this application, administered by a person not specially commissioned from above, have effected the cure? If so, there is no miracle; if not, there is a miracle, but there is a violation of law.

It will be said, however, that if these be violations of law, then law is violated every time that any outward effect is produced by a voluntary act of a human being. Human volition is constantly modifying natural phenomena, not by violating their laws, but by using their laws. Why may not divine volition do the same? The power of volitions over phenomena is itself a law, and one of the earliest known and acknowledged laws of nature. It is true, the human will exercises power over objects in general indirectly, through the direct power which it possesses only over the human muscles. God, however, has direct power not merely over one thing, but over all the objects which he has made. There is, therefore, no more a supposition of violation of law in supposing that events are produced, prevented, or modified by God's action than in the supposition of their being produced, prevented, or modified by man's action. Both are equally in the course of nature, both equally consistent with what we know of the government of all things by law.

Those who thus argue are mostly believers in free will and maintain that every human volition originates a new chain of causation of which it is itself the commencing link, not connected by invariable sequence with any anterior fact. Even, therefore, if a divine interposition did constitute a breaking-in upon the connected chain of events by the introduction of a new originating cause without root in the past, this would be no reason for discrediting it, since every human act of volition does precisely the same. If the one is a breach of law, so are the others. In fact, the reign of law does not extend to the origination of volition.

Those who dispute the free-will theory and regard volition as no exception to the universal law of cause and effect may answer that volitions do not interrupt the chain of causation but carry it on, the connection of cause and effect being of just the same nature between motive and act as between a combination of physical antecedents and a physical consequent. But this, whether true or not, does not really affect the argument, for the interference of human will with the course of nature is only not an exception to law when we include among laws the relation of motive to volition; and by the same rule interference by the divine will would not be an exception either, since we cannot but suppose the Deity in every one of his acts to be determined by motives.

The alleged analogy therefore holds good, but what it proves is only what I have from the first maintained—that divine interference with nature could be proved if we had the same sort of evidence for it which we have for human interferences. The question of antecedent improbability only arises because divine interposition is not certified by the direct evidence of perception, but is always matter of inference, and more or less of speculative inference. And a little consideration will show that in these circumstances the antecedent presumption against the truth of the inference is extremely strong.

When the human will interferes to produce any physical phenomenon, except the movements of the human body, it does so by the employment of means, and is obliged to employ such means as are by their own physical properties sufficent to bring about the effect. Divine interference, by hypothesis, proceeds in a different manner from this: it produces its effects without means, or with such as are in themselves insufficient. In the first case, all the physical phenomena except the first bodily movement are produced in strict conformity to physical causation, while that first movement is traced by positive observation to the cause (the volition) which produced it. In the other case, the event is supposed not to have been produced at all through physical causation, while there is no direct evidence to connect it with any volition. The ground on which it is ascribed to a volition is only negative, because there is no other apparent way of accounting for its existence.

But in this merely speculative explanation there is always another hypothesis possible, viz., that the event may have been produced by physical causes, in a manner not apparent. It may either be due to a law of physical nature not yet known, or to the unknown presence of the conditions necessary for producing it according to some known law. Supposing even that the event supposed to be miraculous does not reach us through the uncertain medium of human testimony but rests on the direct evidence of our own senses, even then, so long as there is no direct evidence of its production by a divine volition, like that we have for the production of bodily movements by human volitions—so long, therefore, as the miraculous character of the event is but an inference from the supposed inadequacy of the laws of physical nature to account for it, so long will the hypothesis of a natural origin for the phenomenon be entitled to preference over that of a supernatural one. The commonest principles of sound judgment forbid us to suppose for any effect a cause of which we have absolutely no experience, unless all those of which we have experience are ascertained to be absent. Now there are few things of which we have more frequent experience than of physical facts which our knowledge does not enable us to account for because they depend either on laws which observation, aided by science, has not yet brought to light, or on facts the presence of which in the particular case is unsuspected by us. Accordingly, when we hear of a prodigy, we always, in these modern times, believe that if it really occurred it was neither the work of God nor of a demon, but the consequence of some unknown natural law or of some hidden fact. Nor is either of these suppositions precluded when, as in the case of a miracle properly so called, the wonderful event seemed to depend upon the will of a human being. It is always possible that there may be at work some undetected law of nature which the wonder-worker may have acquired, consciously or unconsciously, the power of calling into action; or that the wonder may have been wrought (as in the truly extraordinary feats of jugglers) by the employment, unperceived by us, of ordinary laws, which also need not necessarily be a case of voluntary deception; or, lastly, the event may have had no connection with the volition at all, but the coincidence between them may be the effect of craft or accident, the miracle-worker having seemed or affected to produce by his will that which was already about to take place, as if one were to command an eclipse of the sun at the moment when one knew by astronomy that an eclipse was on the point of taking place. In a case of this description, the miracle might be tested by a challenge to repeat it; but it is worthy of remark that recorded miracles were seldom or never put to this test. No miracle-worker seems ever to have made a *practice* of raising the dead; that and the other most signal of the miraculous operations are reported to have been performed only in one or a few isolated cases which may have been either cunningly selected cases or accidental coincidences. There is, in short, nothing to exclude the supposition that every alleged miracle was due to natural causes; and as long as that supposition remains possible, no scientific observer, and no man of ordinary practical judgment, would assume by conjecture a cause which no reason existed for supposing to be real, save the necessity of accounting for something which is sufficiently accounted for without it.

Were we to stop here, the case against miracles might seem to be complete. But on further inspection it will be seen that we cannot, from the above considerations, conclude absolutely that the miraculous theory of the production of a phenomenon ought to be at once rejected. We can conclude only that no extraordinary powers which have ever been alleged to be exercised by any human being over nature can be evidence of miraculous gifts to anyone to whom the existence of a supernatural Being, and his interference in human affairs, is not already a *vera causa*. The existence of God cannot possibly be proved by miracles, for unless a God is already recognized, the apparent miracle can always be accounted for on a more probable hypothesis than that of the interference of a Being of whose very existence it is supposed to be the sole evidence. Thus far Hume's argument is conclusive. But it is far from being equally so when the existence of a Being who created the present order of nature, and, therefore, may well be thought to have power to modify it, is accepted as a fact, or even as a probability resting on independent evidence. Once admit a God, and the production by his direct volition of an effect which in any case owed its origin to his creative will is no longer a purely arbitrary hypothesis to account for the fact, but must be reckoned with as a serious possibility. The question then changes its character, and the decision of it must now rest upon what is known or reasonably surmised as to the manner of God's government of the universe: whether this knowledge or surmise makes it the more probable supposition that the event was brought about by the agencies by which his government is ordinarily carried on, or that it is the result of a special and extraordinary interposition of his will in supersession of those ordinary agencies.

In the first place, then, assuming as a fact the existence and providence of God, the whole of our observation of nature proves to us by incontrovertible evidence that the rule of his government is by means of second causes; that all facts, or at least all physical facts, follow uniformly upon given physical conditions and never occur but when the appropriate collection of physical conditions is realized. I limit the assertion to physical facts in order to leave the case of human volition an open question, though indeed I need not do so; for if the human will is free, it has been left free by the Creator, and is not controlled by him either through second causes or directly, so that, not being governed, it is not a specimen of his mode of government. Whatever he does govern, he governs by second causes. This was not obvious in the infancy of science; it was more and more recognized as the processes of nature were more carefully and accurately examined, until there now remains no class of phenomena of which it is not positively known, save some cases which from their obscurity and complication our scientific processes have not yet been able completely to clear up and disentangle, and in which, therefore, the proof that they also are governed by natural laws could not, in the present state of science, be more complete. The evidence, though merely negative, which these circumstances afford that government by second causes is universal is admitted for all except directly religious purposes to be conclusive. When either a man of science for scientific or a man of the world for practical purposes inquires into an event, he asks himself, what is its cause? and not, has it any natural cause? A man would be laughed at who set down as one of the alternative suppositions that there is no other cause for it than the will of God.

Against this weight of negative evidence we have to set such positive evidence as is produced in attestation of exceptions; in other words, the positive evidences of miracles. And I have already admitted that this evidence might conceivably have been such as to make the exception equally certain with the rule. If we had the direct testimony of our senses to a supernatural fact, it might be as completely authenticated and made certain as any natural one. But we never have. The supernatural character of the fact is always, as I have said, matter of inference and speculation; and the mystery always admits the possibility of a solution not supernatural. To those who already believe in supernatural power, the supernatural hypothesis may appear more probable than the natural one, but only if it accords with what we know or reasonably surmise respecting the ways of the supernatural agent. Now all that we know, from the evidence of nature, concerning his ways, is in harmony with the natural theory and repugnant to the supernatural. There is, therefore, a vast preponderance of probability against a miracle, to counterbalance which would require a very extraordinary and indisputable congruity in the supposed miracle and its circumstances with something which we conceive ourselves to know, or to have grounds for believing, with regard to the divine attributes.

This extraordinary congruity is supposed to exist when the purpose of the miracle is extremely beneficial to mankind, as when it serves to accredit some highly important belief. The goodness of God, it is supposed, affords a high degree of antecedent probability that he would make an exception to his general rule of government for so excellent a purpose. For reasons, however, which have already been entered into, any inference drawn by us from the goodness of God to what he has or has not actually done is to the last degree precarious. If we reason directly from God's goodness to positive facts, no misery nor vice nor crime ought to exist in the world. We can see no reason in God's goodness why if he deviated once from the ordinary system of his government in order to do good to man, he should not have done so on a hundred other occasions; nor why, if the benefit aimed at by some given deviation, such as the revelation of Christianity, was transcendent and unique, that precious gift should only have been vouchsafed after the lapse of many ages; or why, when it was at last given, the evidence of it should have been left open to so much doubt and difficulty. Let it be remembered also that the goodness of God affords no presumption in favor of a deviation from his general system of government unless the good purpose could not have been attained without deviation. If God intended that mankind should receive Christianity, or any other gift, it would have agreed better with all that we know of his government to have made provision in the scheme of creation for its arising at the appointed time by natural development; which, let it be added, all the knowledge we now possess concerning the history of the human mind tends to the conclusion that it actually did.

To all these considerations ought to be added the extremely imperfect nature of the testimony itself which we possess for the miracles, real or supposed, which accompanied the foundation of Christianity and of every other revealed religion. Take it at the best, it is the uncross-examined testimony of extremely ignorant people, credulous as such usually are, honorably credulous when the excellence of the doctrine or just reverence for the teacher makes them eager to believe, unaccustomed to draw the line between the perceptions of sense and what is superinduced upon them by the suggestions of a lively imagination, unversed in the difficult art of deciding between appearance and reality and between the natural and the supernatural, in times, moreover, when no one thought it worth while to contradict any alleged miracle because it was the belief of the age that miracles in themselves proved nothing, since they could be worked by a lying spirit as well as by the spirit of God. Such were the witnesses, and even of them we do not possess the direct testimony; the documents, of date long subsequent, even on the orthodox theory, which contain the only history of these events, very often do not even name the supposed eyewitnesses. They put down (it is but just to admit) the best and least absurd of the wonderful stories such multitudes of which were current among the early Christians; but when they do, exceptionally, name any of the persons who were the subjects or spectators of the miracle, they doubtless draw from tradition and mention those names with which the story was in the popular mind (perhaps accidentally) connected; for whoever has observed the way in which even now a story grows up from some small foundation, taking on additional details at every step, knows well how from being at first anonymous it gets names attached to it, the name of someone by whom perhaps the story has been told being brought into the story itself first as a witness, and still later as a party concerned.

It is also noticeable and is a very important consideration that stories of miracles only grow up among the ignorant and are adopted, if ever, by the educated when they have already become the belief of multitudes. Those which are believed by Protestants all originate in ages and nations in which there was hardly any canon of probability, and miracles were thought to be among the commonest of all phenomena. The Catholic Church, indeed, holds as an article of faith that miracles have never ceased, and new ones continue to be now and then brought forth and believed, even in the present incredulous age—yet if in an incredulous generation, certainly not among the incredulous portion of it, but always among people who, in addition to the most childish ignorance, have grown up (as all do who are educated by the Catholic clergy) trained in the persuasion that it is a duty to believe and a sin to doubt; that it is dangerous to be skeptical about anything which is tendered for belief in the name of the true religion; and that nothing is so contrary to piety as incredulity. But these miracles which no one but a Roman Catholic, and by no means every Roman Catholic, believes rest frequently upon an amount of testimony greatly surpassing that which we possess for any of the early miracles, and superior especially in one of the most essential points—that in many cases the alleged eyewitnesses are known, and we have their story at first-hand.

Thus, then, stands the balance of evidence in respect to the reality of miracles, assuming the existence and government of God to be proved by other evidence. On the one side, the great negative presumption arising from the whole of what the course of nature discloses to us of the divine government, as carried on through second causes and by invariable sequences of physical effects upon constant antecedents. On the other side, a few exceptional instances, attested by evidence not of a character to warrant belief in any facts in the smallest degree unusual or improbable: the eyewitnesses in most cases unknown, in none competent by character or education to scrutinize the real nature of the appearances which they may have seen,[6] and moved, moreover, by a union of the strongest motives which can inspire human beings to persuade, first themselves, and then others, that what they had seen was a miracle. The facts, too, even if faithfully reported, are never incompatible with the supposition that they were either mere coincidences or were produced by natural means, even when no specific conjecture can be made as to those means, which in general it can. The conclusion I draw is that miracles have no claim whatever to the character of historical facts and are wholly invalid as evidences of any revelation.

What can be said with truth on the side of miracles amounts only to this: considering that the order of nature affords some evidence of the reality of a Creator, and of his bearing good will to his creatures though not of its being the sole prompter of his conduct toward them; considering, again, that all the evidence of his existence is evidence also that he is not all-powerful, and considering that in our ignorance of the limits of his power we cannot positively decide that he was able to provide for us by the original plan of creation all the good which it entered into his intentions to bestow upon us, or even to bestow any part of it at any earlier period than that at which we actually received it—considering these things, when we consider further that a gift, extremely precious, came to us which, though facilitated, was not apparently necessitated by what had gone before, but was due, as far as appearances go, to the peculiar mental and moral endowments of one man, and that man openly proclaimed that it did not come from himself but from God through him, then we are entitled to say that there is nothing so inherently impossible or absolutely incredible in this supposition as to preclude anyone from hoping that it may perhaps be true. I say from hoping; I go no further, for I cannot attach any evidentiary value to the testimony even of Christ on such a subject, since he is

6 [Cf. Hume, *op. cit.*, pp. 124-141.]

never said to have declared any evidence of his mission (unless his own interpretations of the prophecies be so considered) except internal conviction; and everybody knows that in prescientific times men always supposed that any unusual faculties which came to them they knew not how were an inspiration from God, the best men always being the readiest to ascribe any honorable peculiarity in themselves to that higher source rather than to their own merits.

PART FIVE

GENERAL RESULT

From the result of the preceding examination of the evidences of theism, and (theism being presupposed) of the evidences of any revelation, it follows that the rational attitude of a thinking mind toward the supernatural, whether in natural or in revealed religion, is that of skepticism as distinguished from belief on the one hand, and from atheism on the other, including, in the present case, under atheism the negative as well as the positive form of disbelief in a God, viz., not only the dogmatic denial of his existence, but the denial that there is any evidence on either side, which for most practical purposes amounts to the same thing as if the existence of a God had been disproved. If we are right in the conclusion to which we have been led by the preceding inquiry, there is evidence, but insufficient for proof, and amounting only to one of the lower degrees of probability. The indication given by such evidence as there is points to the creation, not indeed of the universe, but of the present order of it by an Intelligent Mind whose power over the materials was not absolute, whose love for his creatures was not his sole actuating inducement, but who nevertheless desired their good. The notion of a providential government by an omnipotent Being for the good of his creatures must be entirely dismissed. Even of the continued existence of the Creator we have no other guarantee than that he cannot be subject to the law of death which affects terrestrial beings, since the conditions that produce this liability wherever it is known to exist are of his creating. That this Being, not being omnipotent, may have produced a machinery falling short of his intentions, and which may require the occasional interposition of the Maker's hand, is a supposition not in itself absurd nor impossible, though in none of

the cases in which such interposition is believed to have occurred is the evidence such as could possibly prove it; it remains a simple possibility, which those may dwell on to whom
it yields comfort to suppose that blessings which ordinary human power is inadequate to attain may come not from extraordinary human power, but from the bounty of an intelligence beyond the human, and which continuously cares for
man. The possibility of a life after death rests on the same
footing—of a boon which this powerful Being who wishes well
to man may have the power to grant, and which, if the message alleged to have been sent by him was really sent, he has
actually promised. The whole domain of the supernatural is
thus removed from the region of belief into that of simple
hope, and in that, for anything we can see, it is likely always
to remain; for we can hardly anticipate either that any positive evidence will be acquired of the direct agency of Divine
Benevolence in human destiny, or that any reason will be
discovered for considering the realization of human hopes on
that subject as beyond the pale of possibility.

It is now to be considered whether the indulgence of hope,
in a region of imagination merely in which there is no prospect that any probable grounds of expectation will ever be
obtained, is irrational and ought to be discouraged as a de-
parture from the rational principle of regulating our feelings
as well as opinions strictly by evidence.

This is a point which different thinkers are likely, for a
long time, at least, to decide differently, according to their individual temperament. The principles which ought to govern
the cultivation and the regulation of the imagination—with a
view, on the one hand, of preventing it from disturbing the
rectitude of the intellect and the right direction of the actions
and will, and, on the other hand, of employing it as a power
for increasing the happiness of life and giving elevation to the
character—are a subject which has never yet engaged the serious consideration of philosophers, though some opinion on it
is implied in almost all modes of thinking on human character and education. And I expect that this will hereafter be

regarded as a very important branch of study for practical purposes, and the more in proportion as the weakening of positive beliefs respecting states of existence superior to the human leaves the imagination of higher things less provided with material from the domain of supposed reality. To me it seems that human life, small and confined as it is, and as, considered merely in the present, it is likely to remain even when the progress of material and moral improvement may have freed it from the greater part of its present calamities, stands greatly in need of any wider range and greater height of aspiration for itself and its destination which the exercise of imagination can yield to it without running counter to the evidence of fact; and that it is a part of wisdom to make the most of any, even small, probabilities on this subject, which furnish imagination with any footing to support itself upon. And I am satisfied that the cultivation of such a tendency in the imagination, provided it goes on *pari passu* with the cultivation of severe reason, has no necessary tendency to pervert the judgment, but that it is possible to form a perfectly sober estimate of the evidences on both sides of a question and yet to let the imagination dwell by preference on those possibilities which are at once the most comforting and the most improving, without in the least degree overrating the solidity of the grounds for expecting that these rather than any others will be the possibilities actually realized.

Though this is not in the number of the practical maxims handed down by tradition and recognized as rules for the conduct of life, a great part of the happiness of life depends upon the tacit observance of it. What, for instance, is the meaning of that which is always accounted one of the chief blessings of life, a cheerful disposition? What but the tendency, either from constitution or habit, to dwell chiefly on the brighter side both of the present and of the future? If every aspect, whether agreeable or odious of everything, ought to occupy exactly the same place in our imagination which it fills in fact, and therefore ought to fill in our deliberate reason, what we call a cheerful disposition would be but one of the forms of folly, on a par except in agreeableness with the opposite disposition in which the gloomy and painful view of all things is habitually predominant. But it is not found in practice that those who take life cheerfully are less alive to rational prospects of evil or danger and more careless of making due provision against them than other people. The tendency is rather the other way, for a hopeful disposition gives a spur to the faculties and keeps all the active energies in good working order. When imagination and reason receive each its appropriate culture, they do not succeed in usurping each other's prerogatives. It is not necessary for keeping up our conviction that we must die that we should be always brooding over death. It is far better that we should think no further about what we cannot possibly avert than is required for observing the rules of prudence in regard to our own life and that of others, and fulfilling whatever duties devolve upon us in contemplation of the inevitable event. The way to secure this is not to think perpetually of death, but to think perpetually of our duties and of the rule of life. The true rule of practical wisdom is not that of making all the aspects of things equally prominent in our habitual contemplations, but of giving the greatest prominence to those of their aspects which depend on, or can be modified by, our own conduct. In things which do not depend on us it is not solely for the sake of a more enjoyable life that the habit is desirable of looking at things and at mankind by preference on their pleasant side, it is also in order that we may be able to love them better and work with more heart for their improvement. To what purpose, indeed, should we feed our imagination with the unlovely aspect of persons and things? All *unnecessary* dwelling upon the evils of life is at best a useless expenditure of nervous force: and when I say unnecessary I mean all that is not necessary either in the sense of being unavoidable or in that of being needed for the performance of our duties and for preventing our sense of the reality of those evils from becoming speculative and dim. But if it is often waste of strength to dwell on the evils of life, it is worse than waste to dwell habitually on its meannesses and basenesses. It is necessary to be aware of them; but to live in their contemplation makes it scarcely possible to keep up in oneself a high tone of mind. The imagination and feelings become tuned to a lower pitch; degrading instead of elevating associations become connected with the daily objects and incidents of life and give their color to the thoughts, just as associations of sensuality do in those who indulge freely in that sort of contemplations. Men have often felt what it is to have had their imaginations corrupted by one class of ideas, and I think they must have felt with the same kind of pain how the poetry is taken out of the things fullest of it by mean associations, as when a beautiful air that has been associated with highly poetical words is heard sung with trivial and vulgar ones. All these things are said in mere illustration of the principle that in the regulation of the imagination literal truth of facts is not the only thing to be considered. Truth is the province of reason, and it is by the cultivation of the rational faculty that provision is made for its being known always, and thought of as often as is required by duty and the circumstances of human life. But when the reason is strongly cultivated, the imagination may safely follow its own end and do its best to make life pleasant and lovely inside the castle, in reliance on the fortifications raised and maintained by reason round the outward bounds.

On these principles it appears to me that the indulgence of hope with regard to the government of the universe and the destiny of man after death, while we recognize as a clear truth that we have no ground for more than a hope, is legitimate and philosophically defensible. The beneficial effect of such a hope is far from trifling. It makes life and human nature a far greater thing to the feelings and gives greater strength as well as greater solemnity to all the sentiments which are awakened in us by our fellow creatures and by mankind at large. It allays the sense of that irony of nature which is so painfully felt when we see the exertions and sacrifices of a life culminating in the formation of a wise and noble mind, only to disappear from the world when the time has just arrived at which the world seems about to begin reaping the benefit of it. The truth that life is short and art is long is from of old one of the most discouraging parts of our condition; this hope admits the possibility that the art employed in improving and beautifying the soul itself may avail for good in some other life, even when seemingly useless for this. But the benefit consists less in the presence of any specific hope than in the enlargement of the general scale of the feelings; the loftier aspirations being no longer in the same degree checked and kept down by a sense of the insignificance of human life—by the disastrous feeling of "not worth while." The gain obtained in the increased inducement to cultivate the improvement of character up to the end of life is obvious without being specified.

There is another and a most important exercise of imagination which, in the past and present, has been kept up principally by means of religious belief and which is infinitely precious to mankind, so much so that human excellence greatly depends upon the sufficiency of the provision made for it. This consists of the familiarity of the imagination with the conception of a morally perfect Being, and the habit of taking the approbation of such a Being as the *norma* or standard to which to refer and by which to regulate our own characters and lives. This idealization of our standard of excellence in a person is quite possible, even when that person is conceived as merely imaginary. But religion, since the birth of Christianity, has inculcated the belief that our highest conceptions of combined wisdom and goodness exist in the concrete in a living Being who has his eyes on us and cares for our good. Through the darkest and most corrupt periods Christianity has raised this torch on high—has kept this object of veneration and imitation before the eyes of man. True, the image of perfection has been a most imperfect and, in many respects, a perverting and corrupting one, not only from the low moral ideas of the times, but from the mass of moral contradictions which the deluded worshiper was compelled to swallow by the supposed necessity of complementing the Good Principle with the possession of infinite power. But it is one of the most universal as well as of the most surprising characteristics of human nature, and one of the most speaking proofs of the low stage to which the reason of mankind at large has ever yet advanced, that they are capable of overlooking any amount of either moral or intellectual contradictions and receiving into their minds propositions utterly inconsistent with one another, not only without being shocked by the contradiction, but without preventing both the contradictory beliefs from producing a part, at least, of their natural consequences in the mind. Pious men and women have gone on ascribing to God particular acts and a general course of will and conduct incompatible with even the most ordinary and limited conception of moral goodness, and have had their own ideas of morality, in many important particulars, totally warped and distorted, and notwithstanding this have continued to conceive their God as clothed with all the attributes of the highest ideal goodness which their state of mind enabled them to conceive, and have had their aspirations toward goodness stimulated and encouraged by that conception. And it cannot be questioned that the undoubting belief of the real existence of a Being who realizes our own best ideas of perfection, and of our being in the hands of that Being as the ruler of the universe, gives an increase of force to these feelings beyond what they can receive from reference to a merely ideal conception.

This particular advantage it is not possible for those to enjoy who take a rational view of the nature and amount of the evidence for the existence and attributes of the Creator. On the other hand, they are not encumbered with the moral contradictions which beset every form of religion which aims at justifying in a moral point of view the whole government of the world. They are, therefore, enabled to form a far truer and more consistent conception of ideal goodness than is possible to anyone who thinks it necessary to find ideal goodness in an omnipotent ruler of the world. The power of the Creator once recognized as limited, there is nothing to disprove the supposition that his goodness is complete and that the ideally perfect character in whose likeness we should wish to form ourselves and to whose supposed approbation we refer our actions may have a real existence in a Being to whom we owe all such good as we enjoy.

Above all, the most valuable part of the effect on the character which Christianity has produced by holding up in a Divine Person a standard of excellence and a model for imitation is available even to the absolute unbeliever and can nevermore be lost to humanity. For it is Christ, rather than God, whom Christianity has held up to believers as the pattern of perfection for humanity. It is the God incarnate, more than the God of the Jews or of Nature, who, being idealized, has taken so great and salutary a hold on the modern mind. And whatever else may be taken away from us by rational criticism, Christ is still left—a unique figure, not more unlike all his precursors than all his followers, even those who had the direct benefit of his personal teaching. It is of no use to say that Christ as exhibited in the Gospels is not historical and that we know not how much of what is admirable has been superadded by the tradition of his followers. The tradition of followers suffices to insert any number of marvels and may have inserted all the miracles which he is reputed to have wrought. But who among his disciples or among their proselytes was capable of inventing the sayings ascribed to Jesus or of imagining the life and character revealed in the Gospels? Certainly not the fishermen of Galilee; as certainly not St. Paul, whose character and idiosyncrasies were of a totally different sort; still less the early Christian writers in whom nothing is more evident than that the good which was in them was all derived, as they always professed that it was derived, from the higher source. What *could* be added and interpolated by a disciple we may see in the mystical parts of the Gospel of St. John, matter imported from Philo [1] and the Alexandrian Platonists [2] and put into the mouth of the Saviour in long speeches about himself, such as the other Gospels contain not the slightest vestige of, though pretended to have been delivered on occasions of the deepest interest and when his principal followers were all present; most prominently at the Last Supper. The East was full of men who could have stolen any quantity of this poor stuff, as the multitudinous Oriental sects of Gnostics afterwards did. But about the life and sayings of Jesus there is a stamp of personal originality combined with profundity of insight which, if we abandon the idle expectation of finding scientific precision where something very different was aimed at, must place the Prophet of Nazareth, even in the estimation of those who have no belief in his inspiration, in the very first rank of the men of sublime genius of whom our species can boast. When this pre-eminent genius is combined with the qualities of probably the greatest moral reformer, and martyr to that mission, who ever existed upon earth, religion cannot be said to have made a bad choice in pitching on this man as the ideal representative and guide of humanity; nor, even now, would it be easy, even for an unbeliever, to find a better translation of the rule of virtue from the abstract into the concrete than to endeavor so to live that Christ would approve our life. When to this we add that, to the conception of the rational skeptic, it remains a possibility that Christ actually was what he supposed himself to be—not God, for he never made the smallest pretension to that character and would probably have thought such a pretension as blasphemous as it seemed to the men who condemned him, but a man charged with a special, express, and

---

[1] [Philo Judaeus of Alexandria, *ca.* 20 B.C.-A.D. 50. Assumed the role of chief philosophic exponent of the Jewish religion. His basic intention was to show that Judaism is a philosophic religion consistent with the Greek philosophers, especially in the Platonic tradition.]

[2] [Mill refers to the latter period of the Alexandrian school which, after Plotinus, had degenerated into magic and gnostic speculations.]

unique commission from God to lead mankind to truth and virtue—we may well conclude that the influences of religion on the character which will remain after rational criticism has done its utmost against the evidences of religion are well worth preserving, and that what they lack in direct strength as compared with those of a firmer belief is more than compensated by the greater truth and rectitude of the morality they sanction.

Impressions such as these, though not in themselves amounting to what can properly be called a religion, seem to me excellently fitted to aid and fortify that real, though purely human, religion which sometimes calls itself the Religion of Humanity and sometimes that of Duty. To the other inducements for cultivating a religious devotion to the welfare of our fellow creatures as an obligatory limit to every selfish aim, and an end for the direct promotion of which no sacrifice can be too great, it superadds the feeling that in making this the rule of our life we may be co-operating with the unseen Being to whom we owe all that is enjoyable in life. One elevated feeling this form of religious idea admits of, which is not open to those who believe in the omnipotence of the good principle in the universe: the feeling of helping God—of requiting the good he has given by a voluntary co-operation which he, not being omnipotent, really needs, and by which a somewhat nearer approach may be made to the fulfillment of his purposes. The conditions of human existence are highly favorable to the growth of such a feeling, in as much as a battle is constantly going on in which the humblest human creature is not incapable of taking some part, between the powers of good and those of evil, and in which every, even the smallest, help to the right side has its value in promoting the very slow and often almost insensible progress by which good is gradually gaining ground from evil, yet gaining it so visibly at considerable intervals as to promise the very distant but not uncertain, final victory of Good. To do something during life, on even the humblest scale if nothing more is within reach, toward bringing this consummation ever so little nearer is the most animating and invigorating thought which can inspire a human creature; and that it is destined, with or without supernatural sanctions, to be the religion of the future I cannot entertain a doubt. But it appears to me that supernatural hopes, in the degree and kind in which what I have called rational skepticism does not refuse to sanction them, may still contribute not a little to give to this religion its due ascendancy over the human mind.

APPENDIX

[THE MORAL ATTRIBUTES OF GOD] [1]

The fundamental property of our knowledge of God, Mr. Mansel says, is that we do not and cannot know him as he is in himself: certain persons, therefore, whom he calls Rationalists, he condemns as unphilosophical, when they reject any statement as inconsistent with the character of God. This is a valid answer, as far as words go, to some of the later Transcendentalists—to those who think that we have an intuition of the divine nature; though even as to them it would not be difficult to show that the answer is but skin-deep. But those "Rationalists" who hold, with Mr. Mansel himself, the relativity of human knowledge, are not touched by his reasoning. We cannot know God as he is in himself (they reply); granted: and what then? Can we know man as he is in himself, or matter as it is in itself? We do not claim any other knowledge of God than such as we have of man or of matter. Because I do not know my fellow men, nor any of the powers of nature, as they are in themselves, am I therefore not at liberty to disbelieve anything I hear respecting them as being inconsistent with their character? I know something of Man and Nature, not as they are in themselves, but as they are relatively to us; and it is as relative to us, and not as he is in himself, that I suppose myself to know anything of God. The attributes which I ascribe to him, as goodness, knowledge, power, are all relative. They are attributes (says the rationalist) which my experience enables me to conceive, and which I consider as proved, not absolutely, by an intuition of God, but phenomenally, by his action on the creation, as known through my senses and my rational faculty. These relative attributes, each

1 [From *An Examination of Sir William Hamilton's Philosophy* (3d ed., London, 1867), pp. 119-129. The title "The Moral Attributes of God" has been provided by the present editor.]

of them in an infinite degree, are all I pretend to predicate of
God. When I reject a doctrine as inconsistent with God's nature, it is not as being inconsistent with what God is in himself, but with what he is as manifested to us. If my knowledge
of him is only phenomenal, the assertions which I reject are
phenomenal too. If those assertions are inconsistent with my
relative knowledge of him, it is no answer to say that all my
knowledge of him is relative. That is no more a reason against
disbelieving an alleged fact as unworthy of God, than against
disbelieving another alleged fact as unworthy of Turgot, or
of Washington, whom also I do not know as noumena, but
only as phenomena.

There is but one way for Mr. Mansel out of this difficulty,
and he adopts it. He must maintain, not merely that an absolute being is unknowable in himself, but that the relative
attributes of an absolute being are unknowable likewise. He
must say that we do not know what wisdom, justice, benevolence, mercy, are as they exist in God. Accordingly he does
say so. The following are his direct utterances on the subject:
as an implied doctrine, it pervades his whole argument.

> It is a fact, which experience forces upon us and which it
> is useless, were it possible, to disguise, that the representa-
> tion of God after the model of the highest human morality
> which we are capable of conceiving is not sufficient to ac-
> count for all the phenomena exhibited by the course of his
> natural Providence. The infliction of physical suffering, the
> permission of moral evil, the adversity of the good, the
> prosperity of the wicked, the crimes of the guilty involving
> the misery of the innocent, the tardy appearance and par-
> tial distribution of moral and religious knowledge in the
> world—these are facts which no doubt are reconcilable, we
> know not how, with the infinite goodness of God, but which
> certainly are not to be explained on the supposition that its
> sole and sufficient type is to be found in the finite goodness
> of man.[1]

In other words, it is necessary to suppose that the infinite
goodness ascribed to God is not the goodness which we know

[1] *Limits of Religious Thought,* Preface to the fourth edition, p. 13.

and love in our fellow creatures, distinguished only as infinite in degree, but is different in kind, and another quality altogether. When we call the one finite goodness and the other infinite goodness, we do not mean what the words assert, but something else: we intentionally apply the same name to things which we regard as different.

Accordingly Mr. Mansel combats, as a heresy of his opponents, the opinion that infinite goodness differs only in degree from finite goodness. The notion

> that the attributes of God differ from those of man in degree only, not in kind, and hence that certain mental and moral qualities of which we are immediately conscious in ourselves furnish at the same time a true and adequate image of the infinite perfections of God [2]

(the word "adequate" must have slipped in by inadvertence, since otherwise it would be an inexcusable misrepresentation) he identifies with "the vulgar rationalism which regards the reason of man, in its ordinary and normal operation, as the supreme criterion of religious truth." And in characterizing the mode of arguing of this vulgar rationalism, he declares its principles to be that

> all the excellences of which we are conscious in the creature must necessarily exist in the same manner, though in a higher degree, in the Creator. God is indeed more wise, more just, more merciful, than man; but for that very reason, his wisdom and justice and mercy must contain nothing that is incompatible with the corresponding attributes in their human character.[3]

It is against this doctrine that Mr. Mansel feels called on to make an emphatic protest.

Here, then, I take my stand on the acknowledged principle of logic and of morality that when we mean different things we have no right to call them by the same name and to apply to them the same predicates, moral and intellectual. Language has no meaning for the words "just," "merciful," "be-

[2] *Ibid.*, p. 26.
[3] *Ibid.*, p. 28.

nevolent," save that in which we predicate them of our fellow creatures; and unless that is what we intend to express by them, we have no business to employ the words. If in affirming them of God we do not mean to affirm these very qualities, differing only as greater in degree, we are neither philosophically nor morally entitled to affirm them at all. If it be said that the qualities are the same, but that we cannot conceive them as they are when raised to the infinite, I grant that we cannot adequately conceive them in one of their elements, their infinity. But we can conceive them in their other elements, which are the very same in the infinite as in the finite development. Anything carried to the infinite must have all the properties of the same thing as finite, except those which depend upon the finiteness. Among the many who have said that we cannot conceive infinite space, did any one ever suppose that it is *not* space? that it does not possess all the properties by which space is characterized? Infinite space cannot be cubical or spherical, because these are modes of being bounded: but does any one imagine that in ranging through it we might arrive at some region which was not extended; of which one part was not outside another; where, though no body intervened, motion was impossible; or where the sum of two sides of a triangle was less than the third side? The parallel assertion may be made respecting infinite goodness. What belongs to it either as infinite or as absolute I do not pretend to know; but I know that infinite goodness must be goodness, and that what is not consistent with goodness is not consistent with infinite goodness. If in ascribing goodness to God I do not mean what I mean by goodness; if I do not mean the goodness of which I have some knowledge, but an incomprehensible attribute of an incomprehensible substance, which for aught I know may be a totally different quality from that which I love and venerate—and even must, if Mr. Mansel is to be believed, be in some important particulars opposed to this —what do I mean by calling it goodness? and what reason have I for venerating it? If I know nothing about what the attribute is, I cannot tell that it is a proper object of veneration.

To say that God's goodness may be different in kind from man's goodness, what is it but saying, with a slight change of phraseology, that God may possibly not be good? To assert in words what we do not think in meaning is as suitable a definition as can be given of a moral falsehood. Besides, suppose that certain unknown attributes are ascribed to the Deity in a religion the external evidences of which are so conclusive to my mind as effectually to convince me that it comes from God. Unless I believe God to possess the same moral attributes which I find, in however inferior a degree, in a good man, what ground of assurance have I of God's veracity? All trust in a revelation presupposes a conviction that God's attributes are the same, in all but degree, with the best human attributes.

If, instead of the "glad tidings" that there exists a being in whom all the excellences which the highest human mind can conceive exist in a degree inconceivable to us, I am informed that the world is ruled by a being whose attributes are infinite, but what they are we cannot learn, nor what are the principles of his government, except that "the highest human morality which we are capable of conceiving" does not sanction them—convince me of it, and I will bear my fate as I may. But when I am told that I must believe this, and at the same time call this being by the names which express and affirm the highest human morality, I say in plain terms that I will not. Whatever power such a being may have over me, there is one thing which he shall not do: he shall not compel me to worship him. I will call no being good who is not what I mean when I apply that epithet to my fellow creatures; and if such a being can sentence me to hell for not so calling him, to hell I will go.

Neither is this to set up my own limited intellect as a criterion of divine or of any other wisdom. If a person is wiser and better than myself, not in some unknown and unknowable meaning of the terms, but in their known human acceptation, I am ready to believe that what this person thinks may be true, and that what he does may be right, when, but for the opinion I have of him, I should think otherwise. But this is because I believe that he and I have at bottom the same standard of truth and rule of right, and that he probably understands better than I the facts of the particular case. If I thought it not improbable that his notion of right might be my notion of wrong, I should not defer to his judgment. In like manner, one who sincerely believes in an absolutely good ruler of the world is not warranted in disbelieving any act ascribed to him, merely because the very small part of its circumstances which we can possibly know does not sufficiently justify it. But if what I am told respecting him is of a kind which no facts that can be supposed added to my knowledge could make me perceive to be right; if his alleged ways of dealing with the world are such as no imaginable hypothesis respecting things known to him and unknown to me could make consistent with the goodness and wisdom which I mean when I use the terms, but are in direct contradiction to their signification; then, if the law of contradiction is a law of human thought, I cannot both believe these things, and believe that God is a good and wise being. If I call any being wise or good, not meaning the only qualities which the words import, I am speaking insincerely; I am flattering him by epithets which I fancy that he likes to hear, in the hope of winning him over to my own objects. For it is worthy of remark that the doubt whether words applied to God have their human signification is only felt when the words relate to his moral attributes; it is never heard of in regard to his power. We are never told that God's omnipotence must not be supposed to mean an infinite degree of the power we know in man and nature, and that perhaps it does not mean that he is able to kill us, or consign us to eternal flames. The divine power is always interpreted in a completely human signification, but the divine goodness and justice must be understood to be such only in an unintelligible sense. Is it unfair to surmise that this is because those who speak in the name of God have need of the human conception of his power, since an idea which can overawe and enforce obedience must address itself to real feelings; but are content that his goodness should be conceived only as something inconceivable, because they are so often required to teach doctrines respecting him which conflict irreconcilably with all goodness that we can conceive?

I am anxious to say once more that Mr. Mansel's conclusions do not go the whole length of his arguments, and that he disavows the doctrine that God's justice and goodness are *wholly* different from what human beings understand by the terms. He would, and does, admit that the qualities as conceived by us bear *some likeness* to the justice and goodness which belong to God, since man was made in God's image. But such a semiconcession, which no Christian could avoid making, since without it the whole Christian scheme would be subverted, cannot save him; he is not relieved by it from any difficulties, while it destroys the whole fabric of his argument. This divine goodness, which is said to be a different thing from human goodness, but of which the human conception of goodness is some imperfect reflection or resemblance, does it agree with what men call goodness in the *essence* of the quality—in what *constitutes* it goodness? If it does, the "Rationalists" are right; it is not illicit to reason from the one to the other. If not, the divine attribute, whatever else it may be, is not goodness, and ought not to be called by the name. Unless there be some human conception which agrees with it, no human name can properly be applied to it; it is simply the unknown attribute of a thing unknown; it has no existence in relation to us, we can affirm nothing of it, and owe it no worship. Such is the inevitable alternative.

To conclude: Mr. Mansel has not made out any connection between his philosophical premises and his theological conclusion. The relativity of human knowledge, the uncognoscibility of the absolute, and the contradictions which follow the attempt to conceive a being with all or without any attributes, are no obstacles to our having the same kind of knowledge of God which we have of other things, namely, not as they exist absolutely, but relatively. The proposition, that we cannot conceive the moral attributes of God in such a manner as to be able to affirm of any doctrine or assertion that it is inconsistent with them, has no foundation in the laws of the human mind: while, if admitted, it would not prove that we should ascribe to God attributes bearing the same name as human qualities, but not to be understood in the same sense; it would prove that we ought not to ascribe any moral attributes to God at all, inasmuch as no moral attributes known or conceivable by us are true of him, and we are condemned to absolute ignorance of him as a moral being.

INDEX

Afterlife, *see* Immortality.
Alexandrian Platonism, 85.
Analogical predication, xvi.
Analogy, x, xvi, 19; and design, 28 and *passim*; and miracles, 67; compared with induction, 28, 50.
Anselm, St., xvii.
A priori and a posteriori arguments, 10 ff., 48.
Aquinas, St. Thomas, xvi.
Atheism, 77.
Attributes: divine, xi, xvi, 33 ff., 39 ff., 54 f., 58, 72, 83, 89 ff.; of the soul, 47; relation to substance, 49.
Bacon, Sir Francis, 20
Benevolence, 42 ff.
Bentham, Jeremy, 60.
Bonaventura, St., xvi.
Brain, as set of sensations, 48.
Butler, Bishop Joseph, vii, 58 f.
Campbell, Dr. George, 60.
Causation, 13; and miracles, 65, 68 ff.; and volition, 68.
Christ, as moral ideal, 84 ff.
Christianity, 82 f.; and miracles, 61, 72 f.; God of, 37 f.; Mill's attitude toward, vii.
Clarke, Samuel, vii.
Conditioned, law of, xvii.
Consciousness: argument from, 24 ff.; relation to the brain, 47 ff.
Contrivance: and divine purpose, 40 ff.; and omnipotence, 34 ff., 54; and pleasure, 42 f.; not destructive, 39.
Cousin, Victor, 24.
Darwinism, xi, 31 f.
Deism, 58 f.
Demiurge, ix, 36.
Descartes, Rene, 20, 24.
Design, argument from, x, 27 ff.

Devil, 38.
Ducasse, C. J., xii.
Evidence, 5; a priori and a posteriori, 10 f.; analogical, 28 f.; inductive, 29 f.; internal and external, 59; negative and positive, 49, 62 f., 68, 71, 74; of sense, 61, 67 f., 71; of testimony, 62, 68, 73; second-hand, 73.
Evil, 36, 86, 90.
Evolution, *see* Darwinism.
Eye, anatomy of, 29 f.
Faith, xvi f.
Fénelon, F., 44.
Fetishism, 22.
Final cause, 30.
First cause, argument from, 12 ff.
Fittest, survival of, xi, 31.
Force, conservation of, 14 ff.
Foreknowledge, 37; and miracles, 66.
Free will, 17, 67, 71.
General consent, argument from, 20 ff.
Gnostics, 85.
God: and finite intelligence, xvii f.; and natural law, 9; as fact of consciousness, 26; as first cause, xvii f., 12 ff.; goodness of, 90 ff.; infinity of, xvii f., 92; intelligence of, 33, 36, 63 and *passim*; justice of, 44 f., 90; limitations of, 34 ff., 53 f., 58 f., 77, 83; moral attributes of, xvii, 89 ff.; power of, 34, 54, 89, 94; veracity of, 93; vulgar conception of, 9; will of, 9 f.; wisdom of, 89 f.
Hamilton, Sir William, xvi f., 24.
Hinduism, 6.
Homer, 52.
Hope, 55; and afterlife, 78; and miracles, 75; legitimacy of, 78 ff.
Hume, David, vii, x n., xvi; on de-

sign, x; on miracles, xiii, 60, 62 ff., 70; on polytheism, ix.

Imagination, cultivation of, 79 ff.

Immortality, xii, 46 ff.; basis for belief in, 50 f.; hope for, 81; rewards and punishments in, 55.

Induction, kinds of, 29.

Infinity, 92.

Innate ideas, 21.

Instinct, 51 f.

James, William, xv.

Justice, divine, xii, 44 f.

Kant, Immanuel, xvii; on argument from consciousness, 25 f.; on design, x; on divine power, xi.

Law, double meaning of, 26.

Law of the conditioned, xvii.

Laws of nature: and miracles, 63 ff., 69 ff.; and monotheism, 9; and volition, 67.

Leibniz, G., 10, 20, 27.

Locke, John, 20.

Mansel, Henry, xvi ff., 89 ff.

Matter, nature of, 50; perishability of, 49 f.

McTaggart, J. M. E., xii.

Method of agreement, see Induction.

Mind: and design, 30 and *passim*; as cause, 15; as effect, 18 f.; relation to body, 50.

Miracles, xiii, 56, 61 ff.; and Catholic Church, 74; and divine volition, 65, 68, 70; and human volition, 66, 68; and laws of nature, see Laws of nature; origin of belief in, 74; nature of, 62 f., 65; tests of, 65.

Monotheism, ix, 7 f.

Moral law, 26.

Mysteries, xvi.

Natural religion, vii f., 5; and revelation, 57 f.

Negative evidence, see Evidence.

Newton, Sir Isaac, 20, 44.

Noumena, 90.

Omnipotence, 34 f., 43, 54.

Omniscience, 36, 54.

Optimism, 27, 79 f.

Pain, accidental character of, 42 f.

Paley, William, vii; on design, x, 28.

Paul, St., 84.

Pessimism, 80 f.

Phenomenalism, xii.

Philo, 85.

Plato, 15, 20, 46.

Pleasure: significance of, 42 f.; and divine purpose, 43, 53.

Polytheism, viii, 6 f., 38; Hume on, ix.

Purpose, xi; divine, 39 ff., 53 f., 77.

Rationalism, xvi, 89, 91, 95.

Reason, truths of, 24.

Religion of humanity, 86.

Revelation, xiii, xviii, 57 ff., 93; plausibility of, 59, 72; internal and external evidence of, 59. See also Miracles.

Savages, religious beliefs of, 21 f.

Skepticism, xv, 77, 87.

Socrates, 20, 21.

Soul, as bundle of attributes, 46 f.

Spirits, disembodied, 52 f.

Substance, 49.

Theism: and idealism, 82 ff.; historical attitude toward, 4 f.

Transcendentalism, 89.

Volition, as cause, 15 ff.

Zoroastrianism, 38 n.

The Library of Liberal Arts

Below is a representative selection from The Library of Liberal Arts. This partial listing—taken from the more than 200 scholarly editions of the world's finest literature and philosophy—indicates the scope, nature, and concept of this distinguished series.

AQUINAS, ST. T., The Principles of
    Nature, On Being and
    Essence, On Free Choice,
    and On the Virtues in
    General
ARISTOTLE, Nicomachean Ethics
    On Poetry and Music
    On Poetry and Style
BAYLE, P., Historical and Critical
    Dictionary (Selections)
BERGSON, H., Duration and
    Simultaneity
    Introduction to Metaphysics
BERKELEY, G., Principles,
    Dialogues, *and*
    Philosophical
    Correspondence
    Principles of Human
    Knowledge
    Three Dialogues
    Works on Vision
BOILEAU, N., Selected Criticism
BOLINGBROKE, H., The Idea of a
    Patriot King
BONAVENTURA, ST., The Mind's
    Road to God
BURKE, E., Reflections on the
    Revolution in France
BURKE, K., Permanence and
    Change

CALVIN, J., On God and Political
    Duty
    On the Christian Faith
CROCE, B., Guide to Aesthetics
CICERO, On the Commonwealth
DESCARTES, R., Discourse on
    Method
    Discourse on Method *and*
    Meditations
    Discourse on Method, Optics,
    Geometry, *and*
    Meteorology
    Meditations
    Philosophical Essays
    Rules for the Direction of the
    Mind
DIDEROT, D., Encyclopedia
    (Selections)
    Rameau's Nephew and Other
    Works
DOSTOEVSKI, F., The Grand
    Inquisitor
DRYDEN, J., An Essay of Dramatic
    Poesy and Other Essays
EPICTETUS, The Enchiridion
GOETHE, J., Faust I and II (verse)
    Faust I (prose)
    Faust II (prose)
HEGEL, G., Reason in History
HESIOD, Theogony